REMARKABLE WOMEN

OVERCOMING
Mediocrity©

A unique collection of stories from remarkable women who have created their own lives of significance!

Presented by Christie L. Ruffino

DPWN Publishing

www.DPWNPublishing.com

For more information, contact:
DPWN Publishing
A division of the Dynamic Professional Women's Network, Inc.
1879 N. Neltnor Blvd. #316, West Chicago, IL 60185
www.dpwnpublishing.com
www.ourdpwn.com

Printed in the United States of America

ISBN: 978-1-939794-07-9

Overcoming Mediocrity

Dedication

To every woman who does not believe she can make a difference and to every woman who believes she can move a mountain.

To every woman who continually makes sacrifices for those she loves and to every woman who prioritizes those moments when she can pamper and take care of her own needs.

To every woman who believes that she should settle for the life she has and to every woman who has overcome great odds to create her own life of significance.

To the remarkable women in this book who have shared their stories with you in hopes that their lessons of pain will become your lessons of power.

To the women in my life who believe I am significant and whom I believe are priceless.

Special Dedication

To my amazing mom, Sue Giannini, who had the courage to share her incredible story in this volume in hopes of instilling courage in others and to my wonderful daughter, Jesica Nicole Ruffino, who has worked tirelessly with me on this volume during the final months of her pregnancy and then with a newborn sill ensuring that the project got finished on time and the diapers got changed.

I love you both! <3

The Power of a Story

There is nothing more important in this world than the relationships we build and the legacy we leave in the lives of those who have crossed paths with us on our journey of life. It's the experiences we have along this journey that define our individual uniqueness and creates our own powerful personal blueprint or our unique story snowflake.

It is this blueprint that can empower us to possess a distinct advantage over every other person in this world if leveraged correctly and shared. If we don't have the courage to share our snowflake, it will be lost forever. No one will have the same story and no one can repeat your story. Therefore, those who come after you will never learn anything from what you experienced and what you learned.

I feel that the most significant thing that we can do to add value back into this world is to master the narrative of our lives. All of our leadership and moneymaking ability rests in our ability to discover, craft and deliver our personal story or message in a way that will that allow people to connect to us. The right story shared at the right time with the right person, can alter the trajectory of their life.

However, the most powerful aspect of a story is that we all have the ability to learn from other people's stories. We then have the power to change the direction of the stories we are living to shape our ultimate destinies.

Introduction

Welcome to our fourth in a series of anthology books that are intended to provide women with a platform to share their stories of encouragement, inspiration and prosperity. Our first book, *Overcoming Mediocrity—Dynamic Edition,* was a smashing success. It was released in May 2013 with 22 participating authors sharing their stories meant to inspire other women to succeed. We achieved bestselling status on Amazon in the motivational genre category in only one day. We then duplicated that success with our second Courageous Women Edition that launched in April 2014 and our third Strong Women edition released in May 2015 with subsequent bestselling status achievements.

My initial goal with this project was to build a strong brand and to provide the women of my organization, The Dynamic Professional Women's Network, Inc., with a platform to share their stories. This would allow them to leverage their new author status to gain additional exposure for their business. It would also enable them to receive greater blessings as they collaborated with the other authors to share their stories with a wider audience. It has, however, taken on a life of its own and has made a greater impact than ever anticipated. It is exciting to read the testimonials from women who read the book and connected with one or more of its inspirational stories and then share their own stories on how our books have helped them to make positive changes in their lives.

Because of the overwhelming success of this project, I decided to develop a new vision for this venture which is much larger than the previous one. My new "Exciting, Magical and Wildly Epic Goal" for this project is to have our Overcoming Mediocrity books become main stream reading like the

"Chicken Soup for the Soul" books. I want to have our collection of books become nationally recognized and carried by the big book stores in addition to our current Amazon distribution. I want the authors of the current, past and future volumes to gain increased exposure and greater blessings for aligning themselves with this project so that they can share their stories with larger audiences and make a greater impact.

It is with great honor and pride that I am able to share with you the stories from the remarkable women on the following pages of this book. This is the fourth anthology book in this series. I have had the pleasure of getting to know each of these ladies to learn a little about them and the remarkable stories that they planned to share. I am also deeply inspired by the courage that they are still exhibiting by sharing the personal details of their lives with the sole intention of allowing the reader to learn from their experiences and to possibly spare themselves a little pain. This demonstrates courage and strength as well as showings the humility and heart of a true go-giver. These women, while still on the amazing journey of their lives, all have great things yet to come. They are women who you should know, learn from and emulate.

I am blessed to have had that opportunity.

Christie Ruffino

Table of Contents

Christie Lee Ruffino

Success Evolution

Have you ever thought about what TRUE success looks like to you?

From a distance, it appeared like we were successful; that I was living every girl's Disney fairy-tale life. I married the very cute, yet somewhat mysterious high school bad boy who was 3 years my senior. We had two children together, a boy and then a girl. We bought property and then built the custom house of our dreams together. We had two dogs, one cat, 4 ferrets, 2 motorcycles (his and mine), two jet skis (his and mine) along with a few other toys. We started and then built a very successful auto repair business with multiple locations and we vacationed every winter with and without our kids. People who didn't know us well would think that we had it ALL, but all of our friends and family were watching from a safe distance waiting for the big explosion.

I was only 16 when I began that chapter in my life. Before then, I had been a very shy and introverted teenager who was at first shocked and then proud to have captured the attention of this boy. When the dust settled, and the relationship developed, we got married. I threw myself into being the best wife and mom that I could be. The best was based on what little I knew at that point in my life. But guess what? That explosion finally happened. After 18 years of trying to make things work, it was time to realize that nothing else could be done. In hindsight, I can see how the breakdown of our marriage was just as much my fault as his. However, at the time I was convinced that not one ounce of blame rested on my shoulders. I really thought that I did everything I could to make him happy, not realizing it was a big part of the problem.

Single again, I can remember being in a constant state of anxiety not knowing how I was going to even pay my mortgage every month, let alone all of the utilities, food and other daily living expenses. It was hard to raise and financially support an 8 and 12 year old on my own. However, I thought it would be better to set an example for them as a happy single person, than to have them witness the daily dysfunctionality of our marriage. I can vividly remember the day when I realized that if things didn't change, they would both wind up in similar relationships. However, I wanted more for them than that. It would not be easy, but I knew that I had run out of options. Marriage counseling didn't work. Therefore, it was time for me to be brave, to be single, to start taking care of myself, to create a more stable home for my kids and to start building a new life.

Success comes by choosing what you want most over what you want now.

The next chapter in my life was all about reinvention and finding clear direction. I was already 36 and it was time for me to figure out that childhood question posed to me so many times, "What do you want to do when you grow up, Christie?" Little did I know that it would take me a long time to figure out that answer.

I found myself desperately looking for a job that would pay enough to support myself and my kids. I had never been without a job since I was 15, but my most recent long term position was with my husband's business. Listing my job experience at "Ruffino's Auto Repair" was not very impressive on a resume. Adding to my stress, my x-husband was so angry at me, that he decided it was more satisfying to pay his attorney thousands and thousands of dollars to get out of paying me child support, and it worked. I, therefore, had to figure something out, and figure it out quick. I won't say that it was easy. I had many, many sleepless nights and overwhelming anxiety attacks during my journey, but now I can look back and see how my resiliency paid off. I was determined to make my own money. BUT, more importantly I was determined to find and follow a career path that would be fulfilling. I wanted to be successful. But success to me was not about getting rich. It was about doing something I enjoyed and something that would really help others.

When I was married, success to me was about being the best wife and mom I could. I put my dreams on hold to support the dreams of others. I threw myself into building my husband's business with him, being the best Girl Scout Leader and the most dedicated bleacher sitting Wrestling Mom ever. Now it was my turn. I could finally think about creating the future of my dreams. But what did that look like? And even though success for me has never been money focused, I realized that I needed to make good money to be able to pay the bills that were quickly piling up. I started working with a career coach to work through the uncertainties in my mind and to find a job that would be a good fit for me.

Success comes by following your passion and using the gifts God blessed you with.

I am a creative person. I love to come up with ideas and find solutions for a problem. I thrive when I can make things and tap into my artistic gifts. So when a friend from church connected me to a job as a Processor at a Mortgage Company, I was hesitant. I did not see anything appealing about that job and it was not on the list we came up with during my coaching sessions. How could I sit behind a desk all day and process mortgage documents? How awful!!! The job was, however, at a Christian company, with some great people, which was a plus. An even bigger plus was that it would provide me with a steady paycheck, which was very appealing. Therefore, I accepted.

Things were now chugging along. The drama in our little three person family started to slowly dissipate and life started to become normal, at least normal to us. I got comfortable in my new job and I learned a lot. I took on a bit of guilt, because I did not earn enough money each month to allow my kids to enjoy any extras. We were, you see, living the buy what we "need" plan, not the buy what we "want" plan. But, it was okay because I knew it would eventually get better. I was soon offered the opportunity to transition out of that role and became a loan officer. I liked the idea because the earning capabilities were much greater and I could break free from behind the desk part of the week to attend networking events and find customers. I didn't like the idea, however, because this new job would be a commission only position. This was scary and meant that a bit of drama would be creeping back into my life. I felt, however, that the reward far outweighed the risk, so I accepted.

Success comes by facing your fear and not letting it stop you from anything.

It was not a direct route, but that opportunity started me on a journey that inspired me to eventually build a thriving membership organization, a successful self-publishing company and a foundation to help other women who were in the same position that I was. Success then became focused around helping other women build their own successful businesses through marketing and networking in my community called the Dynamic Professional Women's Network, Inc. My focus then slowly evolved into working with women on a more personal level to help them build their treasured tribe so that they can also find their true success.

As I approach the 10 year anniversary of my journey as the creator of this vibrant community of women, I cannot, in all honesty, say that I never had any regrets. If I did, I would definitely be lying. Time after time, I had to dip into my nest egg just to keep the head of my business above water while its legs were swimming faster and faster under the surface. I had countless days when I just wanted to walk away from it all and get a "JOB" or lose my temper with someone who feels it is okay to be incredibly rude to me or someone on my staff. However, I did my best to remain resilient once again. Sometimes, I would have a meltdown and cry myself into oblivion, but those times got less frequent and less severe as time went on. I became more confident that building this DPWN is God's plan for me and that His plan just can't fail. He challenged me to build a tribe of female business women who want to support each other, so I accepted.

Success comes by uniting
because we are stronger together than we can ever be alone.

Over the years, I have found that the most successful people are those who have learned the art and science of building a successful tribe. They learn how to connect with, support and care about others. They learn how to not only develop their own talents, but they also learn how to discover the talents in others, support their development and collaborate in a way that allows everyone to be more successful than they could be on their own. This is the overall theme of my life and what I discovered on the journey of creating my own life of significance. Within our DPWN tribe, I help entrepreneurs and small business owners, who are new to the business networking world, learn some simple strategies that will bring them tangible and trackable results. I also share some of these relationship networking strategies in my Amazon best-selling book, *Treasured Tribes* which is being offered for a limited time at no cost on my www.ChristieRuffino.com website.

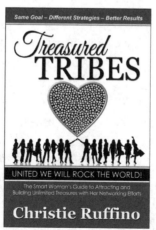

Years later, I can look back and see how every aspect of it all, both the good and the bad, created the perfect foundation for who I am now. I developed strength and determination to be a better creator and leader rather than a follower. I did not have the luxury of being comfortable in a mediocre life. I had to work hard every day, week and month to do more than just pay the monthly bills. I wanted to do more than just get by. I wanted to create a successful business, so I took actions to make that happen. I became an avid learner and consumer of the teachings of the best experts in the industry. I've had dozens of mentors, coaches, advisors and teachers some of whose stories are told on the pages of this book. I created a duplicable system with our Overcoming Mediocrity project to help others share their mastery and message to their ideal audience so that they too can make a bigger impact and help more people in less time and make more money. The women in this book are truly remarkable and their messages were crafted to inspire and equip you to create your own story of success.

I used to have a "block" about money. But, I now BELIEVE that the more money I make, the more people I can serve and the more time I have to spend with my family, my adorable grandchildren and with my friends riding in the wind on our motorcycles. I also learned that I can serve people the best when I figure out who my ideal client is and how I can serve them the most. It is very simple really, but until we figure it out, we just spin our wheels in a never ending journey to find true success. We can't live authentically and appreciate the blessings we have now because we are always focusing on figuring things out for tomorrow.

We have true success when the people who know us the best, respect us the most.

My hope for you is that it does not take you 10 years to find true success; that you get help to figure it out faster than I did, so that you too can create your life of significance and find true success.

Hugs & Blessings
Christie

Christie Lee Ruffino

It was during Christie's journey when she was inspired to create a brand new business called the Dynamic Professional Women's Network, Inc., better known as DPWN. It is an industry exclusive networking organization designed to help women create partnerships with each other to generate ideas, alliances, and revenues within a structured referral generating format. She never intended to start that business to replace the job she was in. Her intentions were only to create a better way to get new customers for that job. However, she recognized the value of relationship networking instead of traditional networking activities and saw the possibility of achieving more success by uniting a small team of powerful, like-minded business women who would invest in helping her as she helped them. And it worked!

A few years later, she transitioned out of her "JOB" to better manage the direction and growth of the organization. There are now referral chapters in many states, along with ever expanding teams of national and international members who meet virtually every month. She then launched a publishing division of the organization as a resource for her members to share their stories so that they could leverage author status and gain increased exposure and credibility for their businesses by participating in one of her Overcoming Mediocrity anthology books or by publishing their own solo-books. Christie also just recently just started a not-for-profit organization in an effort to help other single moms who are going through a temporary life transition, just like she went through, but can't get help by any other traditional means.

In addition to working diligently to ensure the success of the Dynamic Professional Women's Network, DPWN Publishing and the DPWN Angel Foundation, Christie is a past Council Member of the Executives Breakfast Club, served two terms as a Board Director of the Carol Stream Chamber of Commerce, received a 2008 Special Judge's Recognition for the Citizen of the Year award in Carol Stream, in 2009 was awarded a Distinguished Woman of Business Award from American Family Insurance with great pleasure and received her highest honors by being recognized as an Influential Women in Business in 2009 by the Daily Herald Business Ledger and the National Association of Women Business Owners (NAWBO), in 2010 with an Entrepreneurial Excellence Award and in 2015 with a Kane County Women of Distinction Award by Shaw Media.

Christie Lee Ruffino
Dynamic Professional Women's Network, Inc.
1879 N. Neltnor Blvd. #316
West Chicago, IL 60185
630-336-3773
Info@OurDPWN.com
www.OurDPWN.com
www.ChristieRuffino.com

Sue Giannini

A Simple Phrase from Childhood Can Carry You Through Your Entire Life

We tell our children many things; look both ways before crossing the street, if you can't say something nice, don't say anything at all, and don't cross your eyes, they'll stay like that. Some are silly, others are serious about things we hope they'll always remember. We may forget some of them, but others are as clear today as they were when we first heard them in our childhood.

Never Give Up. It was just one of the phrases my father repeated to me as a child. "Never give up, do what you have to do, and if you stumble, never give up."

I grew up during a time when mental illness and depression weren't very well understood. I was the middle child between two brothers. My childhood was happy enough. However, one thing that I didn't understand was why my mother cried so much. She never talked about it. While I loved my mother and yearned to have a close relationship with her, it was difficult for me to get close to something I couldn't understand. I now realize that my mother suffered from depression.

On the other hand, I was very close with my father. The way he raised me was a blessing in my life. He taught me a lot. One lesson that always stayed with me was to *Never Give Up.*

As a child in school, I would whine about the school work. However, he would firmly but lovingly say go and do it. I received good grades thanks to his advice. The one exception was the first semester when I took Algebra and got an F. I wanted to drop the course but he said no, don't give up. Sure enough, I hung in there and in the second semester everything clicked. I even ended up loving the subject.

I had a good adult life. I got married and had two children, a girl and a boy. Of course there were some difficult times like everyone experiences. I got divorced, but unlike many couples, ours was amicable since we had children. We knew it was important to focus on the best outcome for them. Nine years later, I married a man who has been a rock throughout all of our years together.

In 1995, several events in rapid succession nearly knocked me off my feet.

First, my father took his life. If that wasn't a crushing blow, nine days later my younger brother, Chris, also took his life. At the same time, my mother was in the hospital having strokes. I was suddenly thrown into a situation where I felt I had no one to lean on. In addition to handling the shock of these sudden losses and grieving for my father and brother, I was given the responsibility of settling two estates while tending to my mother. This was all in addition to my job, which involved working for an oral surgeon as a dental and anesthetic assistant, with the responsibility of administering IV solutions. Fortunately, I had an understanding boss. Yet I consistently felt overwhelmed and ready to break.

Settling an estate is time consuming and difficult for anyone. In the mid-1990s it still involved paper copies and snail mail. Many of the documents weren't always easy to find. It involved wading through hand-written papers in order to find bank accounts, insurance policies, and other paperwork. This was a slow and often frustrating process. Not only are you dealing with your own grief at the loss of your loved one, but examining their personal papers, will, insurance, bank accounts and other items. This often reveals surprises about someone you thought you were close to.

Another crushing blow came when I discovered that I had a brother who died at birth. He was my parent's first child and only lived three hours after birth. I never knew about him and had no idea where he might be buried. It turned out that he had been cremated and his ashes were still at the mortuary! It was very emotional for me. Who doesn't bury their child? It was a question and new sorrow that I wrestled with in the midst of all the overwhelming pressure.

Settling an estate also opens your eyes to what your siblings are like, especially when there is money involved. Chris and I were close, and it hurt terribly to lose him. However, it was my older brother who dealt another blow. He kept distant despite my pleas for help sorting out not only two estates but the issues involving my mother's care. He only responded when he felt things weren't being handled correctly, leaving me to feel even more alone in the situation.

Meanwhile, my mother continued having strokes. She now needed more care than I could manage while working and handling the estate details. A caretaker was hired so she could stay in her home. She eventually passed in 1998, leaving me reeling from the added responsibility of sorting out her estate. I was met with another surprise. My mother had changed her will, leaving everything to her caretaker. I was not aware at the time that I could have had the situation investigated by senior services. It caused an even bigger split with my older brother who thought I should have done more. This was the straw that broke the camel's back as far as my ability to handle things.

There were so many times when I thought I couldn't do this. *I'll just walk away and let the pieces fall where they may.* But I didn't, I just kept going. When I look back on that time, I think, *how did I get through it all?* It goes back to my father telling me you can do it—and I'm still going on.

I had supportive friends and my husband Larry was a solid rock for me. However, I had difficulty sleeping and began having anxiety attacks. I quickly sank into depression. I knew something was wrong with me. While Larry didn't understand depression, he would sit with me and just listen, holding my hand while I cried. I don't know what I would have done without him.

I knew I needed to learn to calm down and finish the work that I had to do. Depression and mental illness still held a stigma for many people in the 1990s, but fortunately I didn't feel that way. I wasn't too proud to ask for help. I can't say I'm overly religious but I do feel that I got help along the way from something. I knew I needed help, and went to a local crisis center in Lombard.

My story doesn't stop there. Recovering from depression is a process, not an overnight miracle. Over the coming years, I would work with various doctors, each one helping me along this journey. I was so fortunate to find good doctors that I felt comfortable with. There are some that I still see to this day.

Every day I took another step forward. Some of those days, I could only concentrate on just getting through that day. I was hard on myself, especially when I felt I didn't get things accomplished like I wanted to. I would tell myself that it was OK and there's always tomorrow.

I learned that steps in the process are not always permanent. For instance, I started a journal, which is a great tool for many people. Some people keep journals for years. It helped when I first started and was a good way for me to sort things out. Some of the revelations that I had, made me realize I should have done things differently. I ended up feeling disgusted with myself and never went back to journaling.

Thankfully, I kept working with my doctors. My biggest challenge was letting these painful memories go. I would rehash memories and second guess myself 24/7. It was ruining my life. A counselor gave me one of the best techniques for quieting the continual soundtrack that ran in my head. He told me to look at a situation and treat it like a book. I could open that book every once in a while, then close it and put it up on the shelf, leaving it alone until I felt it was the right time to open it again. Initially, I opened those books a lot, because I didn't want to let go of my feelings. But I didn't give up. I opened the book less and less until I finally recognized I was *tired* of looking at this book. It was a simple suggestion, but it made a big difference.

When my husband retired, we bought a cabin on a river in Iowa. The little run down cabin was a savior for both of us. It took us about six months to get it renovated so we could stay in it without working on it. We loved every single minute. We had a ball. We left Chicago every other Thursday and stayed through Monday. It gave me something to look forward to. We loved the area and the people. The cabin held many happy memories that I don't want to forget. Over time, it became too expensive to keep the cabin. However, we still visit our friends there as often as we can.

Those who hear my story find it hard to believe that so many family sorrows, secrets, and surprises didn't completely break me. Looking back now, I realize that I did everything I possibly could. I just kept going. There is no need to be hard on myself. It is difficult to handle situations that you don't want to handle, but that's life. I believe life is a series of tests and you have to pass them one way or another.

Today, I have an optimistic outlook. I've come a long way. It took me a long time, but I'm here. I learned a lot from those horrible, ugly years. I am proud of myself for that. I was so blessed to have a strong, loving husband, and two wonderful, understanding children, grandchildren, and a delightful little great-granddaughter. I attribute my staying power to family, friends, and wonderful doctors.

The simple bit of advice that my father taught me as a child passed on as well. I was there for my own daughter when she faced hard times. During her difficult divorce, I was able to be there for her and encourage her to never give up. I was able to say and believe that things will get better. They always do. Nothing stays the same.

Today, it is easier to find help when you are struggling with depression or just feeling overwhelmed in general by life's difficult moments. You don't have to do it all by yourself. There are some people still out there that don't believe in counseling or therapy—but that is to their own detriment. They'll just go on suffering with their thoughts and memories. Don't be too proud, or afraid to seek help. Reach out, find a good doctor and rely on the people you feel comfortable sharing your story with. I found excellent doctors, some of whom I still see and I continue to see new ones too. They can offer you a way through your pain and provide you with coping strategies and ideas. I can't recommend it highly enough.

And, just for good measure I'll add, Never Give Up.

Sue Giannini

Sue Giannini was born and raised in the Chicago area. She began working for her orthodontist right out of high school. As she became a mother to Christie and Jerry, she was a stay at home mother until they began elementary school. She returned to her position at the orthodontist's office where she especially enjoyed working with the children, who made up the majority of the patient load. A few years later, the orthodontist retired and Sue then joined an oral surgeon. Always fascinated by surgery, Sue obtained a certification in anesthesiology from the University of Chicago. She continued working until her health issues became too challenging. She shares her story of how depression and family secrets and surprises impacted her life.

Sue is retired and lives in the Chicago area with her husband, Larry. While Sue says she'd love to travel the world, she most enjoys her role as wife, mother, grandmother and great grandmother. She is looking forward to the birth of her first great-grandson this fall.

Sue Giannini

630-653-1096

Mikaila Soto

Dying to Live

I would like to start off by thanking you for taking the time to read my chapter. I know that time is valuable and is not to be taken for granted. I'm so grateful to be given the opportunity to share my story among these amazing women in this Overcoming Mediocrity book. Once you read my chapter, you will understand part of my story. As grateful as I am to share part of my life with you, it is my goal to motivate and inspire you the reader. I confess that I did not know the first thing about writing before I was asked to contribute to this book. Once I began, I quickly found out how difficult it is to put my experience into words in a way that will captivate readers. I became very nervous at first. I wanted to call Christie Ruffino from DPWN Publishing and back out of writing my story. Although my experience is my own, every person faces obstacles and challenges that seem downright impossible at times. You have the strength to overcome whatever comes your way, and find success in every corner of your life. I hope that by reading my story it will encourage you to never give up and to always push forward.

Please allow me to introduce myself: My name is Mikaila Soto. I am a mother of two, IFBB Pro, Professional Physique competitor, Certified Personal Trainer and owner of Soto-CPT fitness in Carol Stream, Illinois.

My journey into fitness has not been an easy one. I often hear people make comments that it must be "easy" for me to be fit since I'm a Personal Trainer. Some people believe that it must be my genetics, or that I have time others do not have to exercise. Some people even think I never crave eating certain foods! Rest assured, I have no more time than anyone else. I am human just like everyone else and my body does get sore after training. When I'm out for a nice dinner, I do crave freshly made cotton candy as my dessert. Fitness is not some simple magazine ad claiming to give a person six pack abs in four weeks. One cannot complete a program and then go back to the old habits and routines that got you feeling out of shape and unhealthy.

Living fit and healthy is a lifestyle. It is a decision to change your entire life. It involves making a schedule for all of your activities and holding yourself accountable for both the good and bad choices. It takes some sacrificing on things you were used to. Exercise has to be a priority instead of a chore pushed off to another day when you have time. There is never enough time. You have to make the time. It is not always fun and never easy, but no accomplishment comes without cost. Otherwise, it wouldn't be called an accomplishment.

As unpleasant as all the dieting and exercise may sound, I'm proud of the sacrifice I made to be at the level of fitness that I'm at. In addition to the day to day hard work that it takes to be a Professional Physique Competitor, I have overcome a lifetime of barriers that make me grateful to be a strong woman emotionally, physically and mentally.

I was born as a premature baby, with bronchial disease. Acute asthma can be mild or severe. In my case, it is very severe. Most of my bronchial tubes do not function correctly which causes many health problems. This prevents oxygen from reaching many of my vital organs such as my heart, brain and lungs etc. It has caused even more health problems throughout my childhood and now as an adult. I have often been hospitalized for weeks at a time. It has gotten to the point where they have had to induce a coma so that my body could try to repair and hopefully received enough oxygen through tubes in a ventilator machine to help me breathe and keep my heart running. Growing up with this disease was a very private matter to me. I did not discuss it with anyone. No one outside of my immediate family knew that I suffered from a chronic illness. I never wanted to be a victim or have anyone feel sorry for me due to all the hospitalizations and struggle to stay breathing. When I was old enough to understand, my team of doctors and pulmonary specialists sat down with me and explained my condition to me. As I got older, things worsened. I spent more and more time hospitalized. I had to settle into the realization that I would continue fighting for my breath for the rest of my life.

I bet some of you may think that I must have grown up in a home of health nuts and that we only ate salads and tofu. However, nothing could be further from the truth. I was raised by a single mom in an extended family where I am the youngest of seven siblings. My mother is one of the most courageous and strongest women that I've ever known.

I come from a Latin culture, where in my family it's not uncommon to see many members who don't practice healthy eating or regular exercise. Many are battling their own health issues such as diabetes, hypertension, obesity, high blood pressure etc. Many smoke and have poor eating habits. What can I say, I was raised by an old school Puerto Rican mother. Much of what we eat falls into what I call, "The Puerto Rican diet". I crack myself up. Pernil (Fatty pork meat), deep fried Tostones, rice and beans, a drink called Malta that we used to drink everyday as if it was water, so yummy. These were some of the common foods that we ate.

Once I became a mother myself, I decided that I did not want my boys to grow up in the same unhealthy eating environment that I knew growing up in. Having my family dinner time together was and is important to me, so I made sure we would sit down for dinner together every night. I made an effort and studied nutrition. I learned how to make healthier eating choices. I moved away from buying processed and highly fatty foods. I learned ways to cook healthier meals that we would all enjoy together, as a family. I began to train and work out regularly. After making the commitment to myself to maintain a healthier lifestyle, I noticed positive changes in my quality of life. I felt inspired! I held on to this motivation and worked hard in maintaining a healthy lifestyle. I wanted to be an example to my kids and the rest of the world of what someone can accomplish with commitment and determination. I really believe that people have tremendous potential when they focus. Anyone willing to just push themselves a little out of their comfort zone and work towards their goals—no matter how far out they may seem—can accomplish amazing things. It became my vision to help and motivate others to live a long and healthy life. My vision soon became reality.

It took years of training and discipline to change my physical body. I wanted to help others achieve their fitness goals so I used my knowledge of fitness and designed a business model. I started working as a personal trainer at a local gym. After a couple of years, I gathered a good amount of amazing clients and decided to open a personal fitness studio of my own. Borrowing money and opening lines of credit was never an option. With the crazy amount of hospital bills that I racked up and creditors calling me for payments, there was no way I would ever get approved for a loan. I worked and saved enough money to start my fitness studio, with the help of some loving family that believed in me. They believed that I could manage and work a successful business. Over time, my client list grew. It felt so good to help people and run a successful business at the same time. As busy as I was running my fitness studio and raising two kids, I still focused on staying on track with my own personal training time at the gym. As I said in the beginning of my story, "there is never enough time, you have to make time". I would work 14 hour shifts and as tired as I was, I was still determined to stay on track with my own training. Therefore, I would hit the gym and train myself. At times, I only slept four hours a night. Then I would have to get up and go back to work and run my business. I am so passionate about my studio that I didn't mind losing a bit of sleep as long as I got my own training in and I was able to come to work to help others achieve their fitness goals. A little something I would say when I was ill and not able to get up from my hospital bed, "UNLESS I PUKE FAINT or DIE, KEEP GOING".

Each time I ended up in the hospital, it was harder for my body to recover. I never trained with the intention of becoming a fitness competitor. I trained with my heart and soul just so that I could be in better condition for the next time I had to be hospitalized again. I wanted to be a good role model to prove that my illness wasn't a barrier. I would not use it as an excuse.

Being in the fitness field, I attended many health and fitness conventions and watched many competitions. This is where I learned much about the competition fitness world and met some amazing people that made a big impact in my life. There are a few, that even now after two decades, we continue to be close friends. At a convention called The Arnold Classic is where I discovered an organization called the NPC (National Physique Committee). Two of my closest friends, IFBB Professional Bodybuilder Bill Wilmore and Tony Freeman mentioned to me that I should get on stage and compete. I should remind you that I was never in this field to train myself to compete. All I wanted was to look and feel healthy. As giddy as I was having these professionals tell me that I exemplified the condition of a competitor, I was still uncertain that I was somehow, as we say in "competition shape". Especially with my health condition, I would have never thought I could have trained to the point of sculpting my body to look stage ready. A week later, I had mentioned to an acquaintance that I might consider competing. She sat back and laughed at me, then called her boyfriend over who also laughed in my face and said I had no chance. This was due to my age, being a mother of two, my health condition, etc. I would never make top 5 in an amateur show because these athletes have done what is called (Competition Prep) where the competitors take weeks just to refine their diets and exercise to look competition ready. It was something that I knew nothing about. My feelings were hurt at the thought that they and many at the gym were laughing at me as if it was so far-fetched and that it would be impossible for me. Something like this would discourage many from even going forward with competing. They would just quit before they even started. It's sad to say that many don't understand the force and impact that their words can have on others.

I've been through hell and back with my health issues. However, the warrior in me will never give up. After a few minutes, I took a deep breath and said, not you! Nobody can tell me what I can and can't accomplish. I walked away with my head held high and was determined to prove that with dedication and determination anything is possible. You just have to believe in yourself. I was determined to reach my maximum fitness potential. Of course, as I said earlier, "no accomplishment comes without cost". I am no exception to this fact.

Training for a competition is an exhausting experience, both physically and emotionally. It takes every part of your energy to focus, train properly, eat the right meals at the right times, and still remember where you left your car keys or that I didn't leave the stove on after cooking for the kids. To say, that it is hard to manage a studio, family and training regimen is an understatement. But here's the secret: *When you want something bad enough, and feel your dreams will stay just out of reach, you'll tell yourself "Unless you Puke Faint or Die, KEEP GOING.* So I moved ahead each day with the goal of being a little bit healthier than the day before.

I was determined to do well. I believed in myself when others didn't. The day came when I finally stepped on the NPC stage. Within five shows, I made it to be a National level figure competitor. Shortly after 4–5 National shows, I was honored to earn my IFBB Pro card (International Federation of Bodybuilding). Reaching all of these accomplishments within a year was fairly quick. In this sport, it usually takes years for someone to win their IFBB Pro card. After a year of competing, I was awarded a sponsorship deal with a supplement company. They helped keep me up to date with all of the latest nutritional supplements and promotional gear. Having this sponsorship, made me want to continue competing and doing the best that I could. I didn't want to let anyone down. During the course of my training, my medical condition started acting up. Things got really complicated when I ended up contracting pneumonia. I quickly ended up hospitalized again in the intensive care unit. My lungs and bronchial tubes were shutting down and beginning to fill up with fluid without mercy. I was literally suffocating from within. It felt as if someone was holding a pillow across my face. I felt like I was drowning. It felt as if I was going to die. It was a horrible feeling that I knew too well from my previous hospitalizations. I was forced into the hospital for several days of treatment. The doctors had to induce me into a coma, in order to keep me breathing. Just a few weeks before, I was training to be in peak physical condition. Then in an instant, everything was taken away and I was lying in a hospital bed, being pumped full of morphine with continuous breathing treatments. Many times it would take months for me to recover from something like this. Since I am the only trainer and owner of Soto-Cpt Fitness Studio, there was no one to keep it open for me while I was confined to the hospital bed. I began to lose clients. I eventually had to file for bankruptcy on my business and ended up taking a second mortgage on my home to try to keep the studio doors open.

Since I never told anyone about my condition, those that expected to see me on stage competing began to wonder what happened. My sponsors, friends, clients and pretty much anyone that knew me wondered where I disappeared to. I hated having to share my condition with others and having to release my personal health issues to the public. At that point, I didn't even know if I was going to live another year, yet alone continue to train.

Despite my critical condition as I lay in my hospital bed, I visualized myself competing again. I told the nurses and hospital staff how I would be on stage again. They nodded along as I spoke, trying to refrain from rolling their eyes. I'm sure they thought it was just the morphine drip talking but I knew it was something else within me. The Rebel Warrior inside won't let me quit. It was not always easy to do. My recovery process was painful and slow. I had to be readmitted several times for complications. On three separate occasions, in one year, I contracted shingles—a virus from a reactivation of the chicken pox virus. It is a painful rash that opens up to awful sores that attack your nervous system causing considerable pain. I felt like a monster. Shingles is typically only contracted by the elderly and the young with compromised immune systems. I was admitted into a quarantine room. It is there that I felt the loneliest. I was hospitalized for so long that my legs atrophied and I couldn't even get out of bed to walk to the window and see the outside. There were no windows to view any signs of life outside. Standing was impossible and sitting up was unimaginable. My future was more uncertain than ever. To top it off, I was in a room where anyone who came in had to wear masks and full protective gear, when they came to check on me. I felt like I had been abducted, and I was the alien. By the end of my recovery, I gained nearly seventy-five pounds. I went from one hundred thirty to almost two hundred pounds. I could have cried out that I lost it all and life is hopeless but I didn't. Instead, I found a way to succeed though the agony.

When I began to recover, I was bound to a wheelchair during my recovery. There was a 5K race I had signed up for, prior to my hospital stay. There was no way I could get up and run after what I had been through. I didn't stay at home and feel sorry for myself. I wheeled myself up to the starting line with the help of Vincent Soto, and then pushed my wheelchair with all of my strength. I completed a 5 kilometer race without being able to run. I felt such accomplishment for finishing what I started. I had a new goal now, to get out of my wheelchair and to walk back onto the IFBB Pro competition stage!

Through perseverance and a *lot* of training, winning 1st place was far from what I was necessarily aiming for. All I wanted was to be healthier and able to walk back on stage. Even with my dedication to training, I did not place high in my first few shows. That was not the point. I was just excited to share the stage with such amazing and talented athletes, after all that I went through. The National Physique Competition and the International Federation for Bodybuilding and Fitness gave me a stage to stand on, and a reason to push forward. I am grateful to have had the opportunity to compete in the Tim Gardner IFBB Wings of Strength shows. Throughout my lifetime of tribulations, that year I placed 1st at the Atlantic City IFBB Pro Women's physique qualifying me to compete in the 2015 IFBB Las Vegas Olympia. In our sport, it's like the Olympics, where only the best of the best compete. I was honored to step on that stage where I placed 7th in the World in 2013. And more recently in 2015, I placed 10th and was also awarded the 2015 IFBB Olympia Most Improved Athlete of the Year. I can't even describe the feeling of earning this prestigious award.

I feel compelled to motivate others to never give up and to follow their dreams. I decided to publish a book detailing my personal journey and the necessary steps in obtaining my fitness and health goals. In addition, I describe the importance and fundamentals of how I managed my time with friends and family while running my own business. I am living proof of what can be accomplished with a positive attitude and the will to persevere no matter what the obstacles are.

If you feel inspired by this chapter and would like to be a part of helping me share this with the world by supporting me in publishing my upcoming book, here is my link: https://www.gofundme.com/2k58hx7c

Mikaila Soto

Mikaila Soto comes from a typical Puerto Rican Hispanic household. She was born prematurely with bronchial issues. Mikaila spent most of her teenage years in the Humble Park neighborhood in Chicago IL. High blood pressure and obesity were very common in her family due to the unhealthy Latin food habits. As the mother of two boys, Mikaila knew that she wanted to live a healthier life style. Choosing to be a positive and healthy role model for her boys, she hit the books and became an AFPA (American Fitness Professional Association) Certified Personal Trainer. After several more years of studying, she also became a Certified Post-Rehab Specialist.

Balancing her own Fitness Studio, a business and family made it difficult to pursue a Fitness Competitor career due to her health issues and time constraints. As Mikaila always says, "If you don't have the time, then make the time". She wanted to encourage others that it's never too late to choose a healthy life style. With pure dedication and determination, she decided to prep herself and enter a NPC show as a Figure competitor. With hard work and the support of her love ones, she earned her IFBB Pro card in 2010. Mikaila is a two-time professional OLYMPIAN competitor where only the best of the best qualify to compete in the Las Vegas Olympia Stage. She placed 7th in 2013 and 10th in 2015. She won the prestigious Olympia 2015 Most Improved Athlete of the year award. Competing at the Arnold Classic 2015 were 54 of the top professional WPD Women Physique competitors. Mikaila competed and placed in the top 10.

In early 2011, she became a Sponsored Athlete. After competing in 2011, she was admitted to the hospital with a severe case of pneumonia. She was also diagnosed with bronchial disease which is something that she has been struggling with her entire life. She spent a painful 2 1/2 weeks in the Intensive Care Unit and endured a grueling four month recovery. Mikaila set as her goals to get out of her wheel chair, to continue her journey to stay motivated and to get fit enough to get back on the IFBB Pro competition stage. Mikaila unfortunately continued to be hospitalized several times over the years, even to the point of having to induce coma. She ended up spending as much as three months at a time in the hospital. That didn't stop her from always pushing forward. She truly believed in living life to the fullest, so much that she ended up tattooing it on her right bicep "Live and Love Life

She gets asked all the time about her full sleeve tribal tattoo. She explains that it's not just a tattoo. It's her body art that has special meaning to her. It's her symbol of a true "Warrior". As she adds more to it each time, she is fighting for what she believes in and fighting for her life. She wears it with pride and honor.

"Live and Love Live"

Mikaila Soto
SOTO-CPT Fitness Studio
920 West Army Trail Rd
Carol Stream, IL 60188
630-837-5507
sotocpt@yahoo.com
www.sotocpt.com

Andrea Trovato
Transformation

Life is a culmination of choices, some good, some bad, but in the end, the choices we make transform our lives. Looking back on the roadmap of my life, I've learned that on the route to my destination, sometimes instead of taking one left turn I've had to take three rights but in the end I always wound up right where I was destined to be.

As far back as I can remember, I wanted to be a wife and mother. However, I also wanted to become a nurse and to help people through health and wellness. I guess I've always known that I'm a nurturer. This was an area that was very personal to me since I struggled with my weight from an early age and wanted to learn about nutrition. The signs were clear even then, that I was destined to be involved in this area, but I veered off course and took several detours. For some reason, instead of going into nursing, I chose a different direction and studied law—but the passion to help others never waned. Ultimately, however, the road and the detours led me to where I am today.

When I was 16, my years of yo-yo dieting began, as I lost and regained the same 25-30 pounds. I would spend the next 40 years dieting and certainly learned how to diet, count calories and count points, but I never learned about food from a nutritional standpoint or how food affected your body.

When I moved to South Florida from Connecticut in the 1980's, my road crossed with my husband Ron's. Had I chosen to pursue nursing as I originally had planned, we would have never met. Ron's current position in Florida was being phased out and so when he was offered an opportunity to partner with his best friend in his manufacturing and fabrication business in the Chicagoland area, he jumped at it.

We got married in 1993, when I was 36. And so it began that February morning, when the road led us to Chicago to begin our married life together. It was a typical Midwestern day—cold and windy. It was a big change from my South Florida lifestyle where I had spent the last 10 years. We were married on Valentine's Day and were looking forward to our new life together

That first year was magical. I had left my position as a paralegal and was looking forward to being a stay-at-home wife. We were hoping to start a family immediately. Starting a family in our late 30's was a risk, so we were beyond excited when we learned that we would be expecting our first child later that year. My days were filled with decorating our home and preparing for our new baby. Ron's days were filled with working long days and waiting for the big partnership to materialize. The paychecks were small and the partnership was akin to a fishing lure—something at the end of the line that you couldn't reach. The days passed and the house became a home. However, the job was another story. Was this move a wrong turn?

It was difficult living away from our family and friends. However, we slowly developed a circle of friends and settled into our new lifestyle as Midwesterners. Our daughter, Stephanie, was born in October. She was perfect and pink in every way: ten beautiful tiny toes and fingers and the most beautiful oval face. When I found out I was pregnant again, we were overjoyed. However, the celebration was short lived, since I suffered a miscarriage. I remember my husband bringing Stephanie to the hospital to see me. I clung to her very tightly because I was grateful to have her and didn't think we'd be blessed with more children. Then, I suffered a second miscarriage. When I found out I was pregnant again, I was very excited and grateful.

However, I was extremely nervous and afraid that I would lose this baby too. But God works in mysterious ways, as my Mom would always say, and Ron and I were blessed with Alison, 21 months after Stephanie was born. Michelle came a mere 14 months later. Three beautiful healthy children—my life was perfect!

Our family life was amazing and my dream of being a wife and mother was a reality. Ron was working longer and longer hours and the career move, that at the time made sense, was falling apart. His paychecks were paltry and it was difficult to make ends meet on his salary. Our faith was strong and somehow I knew that we would be ok. The partnership never materialized and the friendship deteriorated. His best friend would NEVER do him wrong, but he did. Did he make the right choice?

It was 1999. I had three small children. Ron and I made the decision to start our own business. Therefore, I was about to re-enter the work force. We made a conscious decision not to put our children in day care. It was a difficult road for several years, juggling three small children and work. Thankfully, my Mom decided to relocate from Florida and move in with us. We had been asking her for years and finally the time was right. Both our Dads had passed years ago and while Ron's Mom had a lot of family around her, my Mom didn't. It was such a blessing to have her with us. In 2003, our world turned upside down when Ron's Mom got really sick. Ron brought her to Chicago so we could take care of her. She had cancer and fought hard but we lost her in three short months. We are a very close family and both Moms got along like sisters. It was tough when she passed. She had given so much to us and we all missed her dearly. This road was a tough one that taught me to appreciate life since it is so precious. It also made me much stronger.

The business was also struggling. It was really hard. The road was very rocky, up and down. But by 2006, it was prospering and we were ready to expand. In 2007, we chose to purchase a much larger building and remodel it. Business was booming! We were on top of the world. As quickly as we were on top of the world, everything went upside down. Shortly after we moved into the new building, the market crashed. Everything we had worked so hard for was just slipping away. I felt like my world spiraling out of control. In order to keep the business doors open and to pay our employees, I had to liquidate our savings, 401K's and everything. It seemed like the minute we closed on that building, everything collapsed. I couldn't sleep at night, gained weight and was miserable. We chose to purchase this building at the absolute worst time. Now what? This was a major road block.

I had to do something to help my family financially. We needed an additional revenue stream. During one of my many sleepless nights, I put the TV on and saw a commercial with a popular TV Dad promoting a company that you could get involved with and sell merchandise. It was a low cost investment with big earnings. "Wow, that's it I thought." The following morning, I called that company up and set up an account and before I knew it I was $10,000 in debt. I joined several chambers and the DPWN and started networking. I really had no idea what I was doing. I was desperate. I started to learn how to promote my business, how to do a 30 and 60 second infomercial and I discovered I liked to present. I also started meeting dynamic women who were entrepreneurial just like me. Many of them were working moms also looking to make a difference for their family. My journey with selling merchandise was a huge flop. However, it was the turn on the road that introduced me to the idea of network marketing. It was a turn that would transform my life.

During this time, I also realized that I had to do more to give back. In a short time, we had lost so much materially. I wanted my children to learn that it was important to help others. Times were tough and many people were losing their jobs and their homes and going hungry. Therefore, we organized events to support the local food pantries. It felt good to help the community and instill some great values in our children. The road was bumpy and twisted, but we stayed the course and pushed on.

The DPWN was hosting an event with Bob Burg and I decided to go. This event would change my life. During Bob's presentation, he started talking about a network marketing company that specialized in creating greeting cards. He mentioned that this company had a great tool where you could send cards from your computer, put pictures in them and build relationships with people. He also talked about people doing business with people they know, like and trust. This was a great way to show appreciation to our RonTro customer base.

As luck would have it, there was a wonderful woman in my DPWN chapter that represented this company so I signed up. "I'm not going to work this as a business", I told her. The rest is history. I started sending these cards with gifts to our customers and they loved the personal touch. People started asking me what I was doing. Before I knew it, I was sharing this service and earning a second income. I earned an award from the company as the second top team builder for 2012. I've since learned to never say never. But as much as I loved this concept and company, something was missing for me.

I just had to find the right opportunity. I read every book on network marketing that I could get my hands on to learn the business model, attended webinars and training sessions and learned from the masters. I wanted to be the best. Surround yourself with leaders and you'll become one. Failure was NEVER an option. Meanwhile, my husband and I continued to fight to keep the business doors open and thankfully, they still are. We've always had unwavering faith and knew that in the end we would be ok. We rented out space twice to two different companies and both of those companies went belly-up leaving us with unpaid rent. This building was just too big for us. The overhead was killing us, but we persevered. The thought of us failing never entered my mind. I knew we would be OK if we just kept going. I'm not going to lie though. It has been extremely tough. We had lost a lot of money, but we didn't lose our family and we had our faith. In fact, our family became stronger and at the end of the day, that's the most important thing. There are so many blessings in my life. My dream was always to be a wife and mother, and that dream was a reality. There were so many lessons learned during these years and in this crazy, tough recessionary market. Through adversity comes our biggest strengths and our kids have grown into amazing young women. They are kind, with strength of character and conviction. To say that I am proud of them would be an understatement. I'm a better person because of them. Did we make the right choices? Had we gone a different route, would our kids be as strong as they are today?

One of the greatest things about network marketing is that you can work from home, the beach or anywhere. Fortunately, I can also do my responsibilities for RonTro from home.

This was a God send when my Mom got sick in early 2014. For 15 years, she lived with us and helped us raise our children. We celebrated together, cried together and travelled together. It was my turn to take care of her. I lost her in January, 2015 when she collapsed in my arms and passed to be with my Dad. She was my dearest friend. This was a very dark time for me. My home felt empty. We all missed her so much. The kids didn't know life without Grandma Jo, because they were very young when she moved in with us.

By June, I was miserable and regained those same 30 pounds. It was now settling in my mid-section like an inner tube. Like many people, I was stressed out. I missed my Mom. I wasn't feeling well. Business was upside down again. I was tired all the time, irritable and had no energy. I decided I that needed to take the weight off again and nothing was working. It was not as easy as it was when I was younger.

When a good friend of mine called me and told me that she was doing a 10-day transformation, I was curious and desperate. She told me that the program was designed to cleanse your body from all the processed junk that we're accustomed to eating and drinking. The bonus side effect was a 5–20 pound weight loss on average. "You can do it for 10 days", I thought. This was the network marketing opportunity I longed for, but at first I didn't see it. In fact, I said to her, "I'm not doing the business." Remember, how I said before never say never? I took off 8 pounds in 10 days and was motivated to continue with the weight loss products. My mood started shifting and I felt energized. I woke up feeling amazing and I slept better. My oldest daughter who had gained weight in high school and college after injuring her ACL in the 8th grade asked me "Mom, what are you doing? Your energy is off the hook. Can I do it?" At first I told her, "Honey I don't think you can give up bread for 10 days." She said, "Mom, I can do anything for 10 days." By end of 60 days, I was down 21 pounds and within 6 months 300 pounds. My daughter took off

40 lbs. and felt so good about herself. I felt amazing and felt a responsibility to share this program with others. Therefore, I started sharing my results and started building my dream business. After 6 months, my husband jumped on board and took off 38 pounds that he had gained through 24 years of marriage. My two other daughters joined the program for good nutrition. They also love the lifestyle. This has become our family's lifestyle. I am very thankful to be able to share this gift of health with them.

Joining Purium has been the realization and fulfillment of one of my life-long dreams. It has been like coming full circle. The choices I have made through the years, have brought me to a place that I was destined to be right from the beginning. I just had to be willing to claim it and trust in myself. Therefore, last June when I made the choice to join Purium and reclaim my life, I made a huge step forward in entering the health and wellness area – my destiny.

I've learned that "diet" is a 4-letter word. There is no more counting calories or points, but living a life-style with foods that are grown organically, without genetically modified ingredients. Our products are Certified Organic, Vegan, Gluten-Free, have no-GMO's and are Certified Kosher too. I've learned why that's important and I've helped hundreds of people realize that as well. My next step is to take extensive nutritional training classes through my company, so I can continue to fulfill my dream of helping people live their healthiest life possible. It's an amazing feeling to help people feel better and be the best they can be.

As I write this, our building is under contract and we hope to close in early September. We'll be able to walk away whole and downsize. The road has been tough and it has taken turns that at times felt like I had driven off of it. Have I made the right choices? Have I made the right turns? In retrospect - absolutely, no regrets.

The choices we make transform our lives…and can transform others as well.

Andrea Trovato

Andrea Trovato is a Business Owner, Entrepreneur, Public Speaker and Home Based Business Professional. She has been co-owner and President of RonTro Enterprises, a metal precision laser cutting company since 1999. A native of New York City, she now lives in Chicago with her husband Ron and their three daughters. Trovato's early paralegal background proved helpful for business development.

For the last seven years, Andrea has excelled in the Home Based Business, specifically in Network Marketing by using the philosophy of leveraging time and resources. In this recessionary market, she knew additional income was integral in sustaining long term financial stability for her family. Most notable was her ability to help grow a European company, by recruiting, training and motivating a team of 1500 marketers in 9 different countries.

When Trovato was offered an opportunity to expand income and growth potential with Purium Health Products in the USA, she quickly took on a leadership role. This was a win-win decision for the promotion of a healthy lifestyle and recognizing the perfect timing of a rising Fortune 500 star in health, beauty and Superfood nutrition. This marketing model provided a powerful way to become a success and to pay it forward to help others build better health and wealth. In a few short months, she achieved the Diamond rank and won a leadership trip to California. She is a walking billboard based on the belief that what you put in your body will determine how you look, feel and perform. The Purium 20 Point Commitment to purity and potency and a commitment to 100% non-GMO products is a logical generational choice for any health conscious family.

As a speaker for audiences in the thousands, Trovato has also appeared on CEO Intronet TV Show, The American Businessperson Radio, The Daily Herald and WGN Radio with Bill Moller.

Andrea Trovato
Purium Health Products
Diamond Executive Distributor
630-327-4460
andrea@andreatrovato.com
www.andreatrovato.com

Courtney Powell
Life After Debt

As a child, I wasn't quite sure what I wanted to be when I grew up. That could have been because my mother focused on telling me that I needed an education, period. There was no pressure to become a lawyer or a nurse, simply get an education. And so I did. I graduated from high school and went on to college to earn a bachelor's degree and then a master's degree. However, what I didn't realize was that along the way, I also picked up some lessons on how to mismanage my finances. I was inadvertently educated in the ways of borrowing money in the form of using credit cards, when I didn't want to use my own funds or just didn't have the money to buy what I wanted. I first learned this at home and these lessons were later validated. I made it a part of how I lived as I observed my friends and relatives doing the same things. This was the beginning of the faulty foundation that my idea of personal financial management would be built on.

My earliest memory of using the "credit crutch" came in the form of a shopping spree I went on as I prepared to go back to school in the fall. Of course, I had to have new clothes. I went out with my brand new credit card in hand. I spent somewhere around $300 and whenever my minimum payments gave me a bit of margin, I'd use the card for something else. These were never necessities. It was just whatever I wanted to buy for myself or someone else.

I initially attended college on an academic scholarship but because of my poor habits and choices that was lost. As a result, I had to pay for my education. Yes, as you may have guessed, this is how I was introduced to student loans. I soon found out that it was common to borrow more than was needed to pay for tuition, books and related fees. The rationale was to save the excess funds. However, what actually happened is that the excess money is what I used to continue with my spontaneous spending and making minimum credit card payments. That "smart" move set me up for over a decade of loan payments after I'd graduated. It didn't bother me then because I thought that's how life was supposed to be. Everyone I knew had several credit card bills to pay each month.

I graduated, made my mother proud and got my first "real" job. I enjoyed the work and it soon became my world. I had no life outside of that job. That was my choice because I had dreams of moving up the corporate ladder. My focus was "What's in it for me?" and "How can I get ahead?" I had my own apartment, a nice car, a good job and felt like I was living the dream. However, the debt continued to pile up.

But then life presented me with another opportunity. I met a wonderful guy through a mutual friend. We were engaged the next year and got married the following year. We decided to build our first house and moved in about 6 months after we married. While we were saving for the down payment for the house, we managed to pay off my husband's debt. However, my debt still remained. My world now got a little bigger…with a new husband and a new house that required both of our salaries just to cover our expenses. We were so happy to be making our own way in the world and it was just us for several years. We were very active in our church and working hard in our corporate jobs. We'd agreed that when we started a family, I'd stay home if I wanted to. When our son was born, that's what I did. At that point, my son became my world and I was glad to be able to stay home with him.

Babies have a way of changing everything. Our focus was now pretty much centered on him. We had to decide what we would do, where we would go and how we could raise our perfect little boy. Then baby number two came, our daughter. Our family grew and we began to realize there was so much that we wanted to do and experience as a family. We combined our resources with some friends and decided to invest in residential real estate.

We thought it would provide us with the stability that we would need to make that extra income that we needed to do all of the things that we dreamed about and to keep up with the credit card and loan payments. We were wrong.

I think investing in real estate is a good idea. However, at that time, we simply were not ready to be hands-on investors. In 2006, the economy started to decline and we never saw it coming. By that time, we were invested in our own home and a couple of other properties. One was a single family home with a tenant and the other was a townhouse that we were trying to "flip". We sank pretty much all of our money into the purchase and fixing up of these properties. There were no reserve funds and no exit strategy. The money started to get really tight really fast, so we fell back on increased use of our credit cards until we were living off of them. We decided to sell the properties as quickly as we could and finally did, but we made none of the profit that we anticipated. Our attention now turned to our own home mortgage payments which had been falling behind along with the other bills.

We hoped and prayed and did everything we knew to do to get out of the financial hole we were in and nothing worked. We were occasionally able to get an extension here or a forbearance but it was a constant struggle. The bank that held our mortgage was unwilling to help us. Our money issues became the usual topic of conversation and were starting to take center stage—at least for me. The money stuff was always on my mind. I finally looked at the situation and the stress it was causing and decided that enough was enough. We were focusing most of our time and energy on holding onto what really amounted to a pile of wood, copper, plastic and metal and for what reason? It was obvious that without some miraculous act, we would not be able to stay in our home. I was no longer willing to continue to put my family through this stress. We had to make a choice between the house and our family's well-being. In the end, we walked away from the only home our children had known. But the positive side of the experience was that my husband and I were able to emotionally divest from all of the material things we'd collected over the years.

We were able to move to another house near my husband's job at that time and started to put our lives back together. Several months later, my husband was laid off after 17 years of employment. It was something that we never expected to happen. Fortunately, he was given a good severance package and just as those benefits were about to end 11 months later, he found a job.

The next few years were harder than we thought possible. I never imagined having to go through anything like this. Most people never knew what was happening. As tough as things were, I can honestly say that my husband and I never argued and he never blamed me for the mess we had gotten into. But I blamed myself and felt that I was the reason my family was struggling. This was one of the lowest times in my life but it caused me to take a long, hard look at how I'd been living. It was during this experience and the recovery process that I started to question everything my life had been focused on. I realized that there were some things I'd never learned growing up and that lack of knowledge ultimately led to the poor decisions and mixed up priorities that had gotten me into financial trouble. The concepts of saving (and actually not touching the money) and delayed gratification were completely foreign to me. I grew up financially illiterate and never knew it. As I observed everyone in my community, I saw that this was the norm and I fell right in step with everyone else.

This was a huge eye-opener that led me to determine that I would do all that I could to never get into this situation again. I wanted to teach my children how to manage their money responsibly so they'd never have to experience what I did. But there was an even bigger a-ha moment for me that has changed the course of my life.

As I considered how my upbringing and cultural norms influenced my perspective and behavior, I wished that someone would have taught me how to handle money and credit responsibly. Of course, the information was available for someone actively looking for it. But I wasn't looking for it. While I was growing up, I didn't even know that information existed. I certainly didn't understand that what I was witnessing in my little corner of the world would lead me off a financial cliff in the years to come. If I only knew then, what I know now!

I decided that I wanted to provide the information to others regarding personal finance and life management skills that I didn't receive. I spent many hours considering how to make this information available and to what group of people. As I looked back over the pattern of my life, I noticed what I was naturally good at and what I enjoyed. I realized how others seemed to gravitate towards me for guidance and advice. It was then that I uncovered my mission and my unique purpose. After continuing to research and share my thoughts with my husband, who was and still is totally supportive, I decided to start a life coaching practice to encourage, motivate and inspire others to live their lives by design instead of default. I firmly believe that every person on this planet was created on purpose for a purpose. The sooner we can figure out what it is, the more people we can serve. The more I thought and prayed about life coaching, the more that I knew it was the right path for me.

Since that time, I've been committed to leveraging my background in Human Resources and Marketing to build a business dedicated to helping professional women at all levels connect with their specific and unique purpose so they can lead authentically and serve joyfully in their calling.

So…what about you? If I asked you if you felt like you're living fully in your God-given purpose, how would you answer? Would you be able to respond immediately and enthusiastically in the affirmative? Would you be able to recall the milestones and patterns of your life that led you to that "aha" moment when you finally saw your life's mission clearly? Would you still light up whenever you told the story…even after what seemed like the millionth time?

You have no idea how much I want your answer to be "YES!"

But maybe your answer is more like what I often hear:

"I'm tired of just going through the motions..."

"The years are passing by and I just feel like I'm stuck..."

"I don't even know where to start..."

"I know what I want to do but getting things aligned to get what I want out of life is a different story."

What I have to say next is very important...critical, even. I want you to pay close attention. YOU ARE STRONG. YOU ARE BEAUTIFUL. YOU ARE SMART. YOU ARE POWERFUL. YOU ARE ENOUGH.

I want you to re-read that sentence and this time make it personal. Replace "you are" with "I am" and say it out loud. This may seem like a small thing but this is how you begin to shift your mindset from what you can't do and don't have, to what you CAN do and DO have.

Always remember the wisdom of the bible passage: All things are possible to those who believe.

What do you really believe?

Courtney Powell

As a Lifestyle Strategist, Courtney uses a purpose-driven approach to help busy women-preneurs simplify their lives so they can lead authentically and serve joyfully in their calling.

Courtney's life coaching practice is anchored in the idea that everyone was created with a specific and unique purpose to accomplish. She was inspired to become a life coach after overcoming hardship, overwhelm and personal brokenness in her own life. God has taken her on a faith adventure that has caused her to experience breakthroughs that she never thought possible. He also taught her important life lessons that she feels compelled to share with others. Courtney engages others in a passionate way that causes them to consider the hand of God on their lives and to move forward in order to fulfill their deepest desires for a meaningful life.

Courtney's professional background includes a Bachelor's degree in Marketing, a Master's degree in Human Resources Management and 15 years of corporate experience in Human Resources. The "corporate trenches" is where she developed her coaching skills to assist employees at all levels in navigating various workplace issues. This combination of training and experience (personal and professional) equips Courtney with the skills, understanding and "tough love" approach to guide the overwhelmed, overworked and overcommitted to a place of peace where they intentionally design, not only a fulfilling life, but a lasting legacy.

Courtney currently serves as the DPWN West Chicago Chapter Director. She holds membership in the National Association of Professional Women. She also leads a mastermind group for Christian women business owners.

Courtney Powell
Lifestyle Strategist and Purpose Coach
courtney@courtneypowellonpurpose.com
www.courtneypowellonpurpose.com

Deborah Knight

Accelerating Women's Careers: How Passion, Purpose, and Planning are Changing Lives

"For I know the plans I have for you," declares the Lord, "plans to prosper you and not to harm you, plans to give you hope and a future." —Jeremiah 29:11

When I set up the conference room for the first Women's Executive Club (WEC) meeting, I wasn't sure what was going to happen, however, I knew that it was going to be good. It was a small group, of just a dozen women, but their energy and enthusiasm lit up the room. I told them what WEC would do for them: accelerate their careers by bringing together high-achieving professional women to connect with one another, learn best practices, hone their leadership skills, and belong to a community of like-minded professionals. Apparently, they saw the same potential that I knew was there—eleven of the twelve joined on the spot, and the WEC was off and running!

I was taking a big risk when I quit what was a secure, steady job in financial services to fully invest myself in WEC. Today, I am blessed to be doing work that I absolutely love. I help women executives, professionals, and business owners excel professionally and advance their business by providing the right connections, knowledge, and resources. My work means turning my passion and a very clear need into a reality for professional women who can't find this in any other organization.

A Very Real Need for Women at the Top

In a way, WEC was something I wish I'd had for my own career. From the time I was a student, to my legal career, and then my work in financial services, being a high-achieving woman makes you stand out. You're driven to perform. You want to achieve, score the top awards, and excel at everything that you do. Maybe you're competitive, or maybe you just want to do your best every single time. But you put in the hours it takes to do a job right, and you're committed to doing it right every single time.

When I got into legal work, I won my first jury trial after just two months at the firm. I had no problem litigating civil lawsuits in front of judges and juries, and I especially took pride in winning my cases. The fourteen-hour days, hours of research, piles of paperwork…no matter what it took, every time I walked into a courtroom, I had full confidence in my abilities. It wasn't about winning—it was about simply doing my best. Usually, that was good news for my clients, too.

Even back then, I started to get a sense for the needs that WEC would address for its members. I learned this the hard way when I approached my managing attorney about changing my schedule. On one hand, I had a career that I loved, but I was putting in fourteen-hour days. On the other hand, I had a young son at home that needed to see more of his mother. At the time, I was doing really well and intended to keep it that way. But I needed something to change. I went to my managing attorney and asked if I could work four days a week (this meant cutting back to an average of about 60 hours a week) or if we could get another paralegal to help out with some of the paperwork.

His answer: "Maybe, in three or four years."

Of course, his hope was that I would forget about that when my son was old enough for school. But I wasn't going to forget, and I certainly wasn't going to prioritize my work over my son for another "three or four years." I decided to resign.

Later, when I switched to a career in financial services, I had to bring in \$15 million in client money in two years—or I was going to get the boot. I knew I could do it—so I sat down, made a plan, and stuck with it. It was two years of crazy. I was switching gears fast and discovering new gears that I never knew I had! But the plan worked: while most of my colleagues were leaving every quarter because they didn't meet quota, I had met my goal of bringing in \$15 million in client money—and I did it six months ahead of schedule. What's more, I did it on my terms. I had promised myself that my work was not going to get between me and being there for my son—so for every one of his school or sporting events, I was there.

I've always had this drive and passion. Over and over again, people tell me it shines through no matter what I do. I never realized how critical this drive would be until I started my own company. Of course, the excellent professional experience I had accumulated was also crucial.

I have always loved challenging, high-stakes work. But I noticed something as I climbed the ranks. For one, there wasn't a whole lot of camaraderie for high-achieving women in traditionally male-dominated industries. They say it's lonely at the top—but it's a completely different kind of lonely if you don't share a lot of the same experiences and challenges as your work peers. As a divorced mother, my day looked really different from most of my male co-workers. I had more demands on my time. When I left my day at work, I had a whole other shift to work at home. I felt like I had no professional peers who could understand the challenges I faced, and offer insights for dealing with this kind of situation.

I again saw that there was a need for what I later created in WEC: *a space where high-performing women could talk about their challenges in work and their life outside of work.* Sure, there were professional groups that brought together women within specific industries and across professions. But nothing was specifically targeting professional women, in the upper echelons of medicine, law, engineering, accounting, and for women directors and C-suite executives in other high-pressure industries.

What WEC Does For Women: Best Practices, Great Connections, Professional Development

I knew God was calling me to start a business that would do just that—give driven professional women an organization that recognized their challenges, offered professional development, networking, and benefits to their businesses and industries. They needed a group where they could find the resources to succeed at a high level, and meet with other women they could relate to professionally. This was a big idea—and definitely nothing I had ever planned for myself. However, I knew that this was God's plan, and it was up to me to make it happen.

While I was still working at the time as an advisor for a large bank, it didn't stop me from going full-speed on my WEC plans. I asked our current members to tell other professional women and entrepreneurs about WEC, and to spread the word about what they experienced. In those first few months, I held a kick-off celebration, with ninety women in attendance. The word had clearly got around! Members were telling me that they wished they'd had something like this years ago. I can't tell you how many times I've told another woman about WEC, and she has said, "Wow! I've been searching for something like that for years!" One woman joins, and her company sends in a few more women, because they see the benefit immediately. Before long, I knew that my plan for WEC going national was going to be a reality. At every meeting, women said that WEC was filling a gap that wasn't being addressed anywhere else.

Within the first few months, WEC had members in Atlanta, Seattle, and Chicago. I was very excited about this. However, I knew that I wanted to hone the group here first. I let growth happen organically, and focused on developing the strongest, most valuable program I could for WEC in Kansas City, while developing a plan for scaling to other cities.

It was critical to me that WEC offer what women could not find elsewhere. WEC had to be unlike any other kind of professional or networking group for women or for a particular industry. For example, once a month we'd have a social event at a woman-owned business. Those events were definitely helpful in building relationships and making the group more than just a professional resource.

One of my more controversial changes to the group's structure proved to be one of the most successful. While WEC was initially industry exclusive, I decided that a more cooperative approach would benefit the group more. Rather than just having one doctor, or one intellectual property attorney, WEC would permit more than one professional from an industry to become a member. Initially some women said that they wanted the group to stay industry exclusive, but just a few months later, they were telling me how glad they were to meet other women in their same industries, but on different career tracks and with different companies! It was a good move and really helped to expand our members' networks. Furthermore, it showed me that the best entrepreneurs are the ones who anticipate the needs of their clients and take risks, despite what the polls say!

Of course, one of the core principles of WEC is sharing best practices, ideas, and resources. One of the ways we do it is by bringing in speakers or speaker panels to talk about industry best practices and trends. It is true that many groups feature speakers, but we also incorporate discussion and reflection. After a table hears a speaker and discusses key questions, a spokeswoman will share each table's insights with the rest of the group. These "mastermind discussions", as we call them, have been a great opportunity for members to expand their resources and make better connections with the rest of the group.

For our members, the benefits of WEC are more than just the boost to their career. It's also about getting the support and relationships from other women who "get it." For women in top-notch careers, there's so much pressure to deal with. And when women like that are able to come together, help each other solve problems, make the connections that matter, and accelerate their own careers, it's an incredible experience.

I think some of our own members have said it best:

> *"For my career, it was important to network strategically. My free time is limited, so I need a group that offers business development opportunities as well as camaraderie. WEC fits that bill. The diversity and quality of women in this group is exceptional. These women have been an excellent source of business, mentorship, and friendship."*
>
> *—Attorney-at-law*

> *"...the message from the Women's Empowerment Event helped me to make positive changes and start my own business."*
>
> *—Entrepreneur*

> *"I saw Women's Executive Club as an opportunity to network with other women in leadership positions. Not only have I been able to do just that, but I've been impressed with the WEC meetings and the panel presentations, which are always fun and informative!"*
>
> *—Medical Leader*

> *"...The women I have met are talented, successful, and committed to supporting other women!...I definitely recommend WEC membership to other professional women."*
>
> *—Executive at Fortune 500 companies, former; Author, Speaker, & Consultant*

> *"I joined WEC because I was interested in meeting other professional women and expanding my personal network. After my first session, I knew there would be high quality members joining this club. Ever since that meeting, I have formed friendships and contacts that are quite valuable to me in both my personal and professional life."*
>
> *—Broker/Owner*

"It's so difficult as busy entrepreneurs to make time for vital friendships outside of work life. I'd heard about WEC, and my friend had suggested that if only one or two new connections were made on a personal or professional level, the club would be worth the value. My first visit, I joined on the spot. The mix of successful professionals, the fascinating meeting topic, the food, and the venue—it was a wonderful platform for mingling, mentoring, and making new connections. Not only did I find these women of WEC inspiring, considering their stature and successes in their fields, but they were incredibly approachable as well!"

—Business Owner

Plans to Prosper: A Bigger Future for WEC

I ask for, and listen to members' feedback because I know WEC will be an ever-evolving association with a BIG Future. The great news is that even in our early stages WEC is fulfilling a set of critical needs for our members. WEC is providing the "right" connections, knowledge, and resources that are otherwise missing for women who want to excel professionally and accelerate their careers.

Women from multiple other states are already asking me to expand WEC to their cities. I am now launching new WEC Chapters, standardizing our processes, and building a new website to make it easy for you to start and lead a chapter of WEC in your city.

I started WEC with a question—could there be an organization for high-performing women professionals that offered camaraderie, insight, and career development?

Now, my question is—What can WEC do for you? And what can WEC do in your city?

If WEC sounds like a group you want to be part of, or if my story that led to WEC resonates with you, then I invite you to join us on this exciting journey for professional women!

Please talk with us about what WEC can do to accelerate success for you and your community.

Call Debbie at (913) 449-4996, or email her at president@WomensEC.com.

Learn more about WEC at www.WomensEC.com

Deborah Knight

Deborah Knight J.D. is the Founder and President of Women's Executive Club (WEC), LLC. The club is a professional organization exclusively for women executives, professionals, and business owners. It offers its members the right connections, knowledge, and resources to accelerate their careers.

Ms. Knight's professional career began at the University of Kansas, where she earned a B.S. degree in Business. She later returned to earn a J.D. from the University of Kansas School of Law, which she completed in a two-year accelerated program.

Prior to founding WEC, Ms. Knight enjoyed a career as a successful trial attorney and also worked as an advisor for two Fortune 500 financial firms. Her interest in helping other professional women and business owners stemmed from her own experiences in overcoming obstacles in traditionally male-dominated industries. Furthermore, as a divorced mother, busy professional, and entrepreneur, she knew that it was important to have a network of peers to access the right connections, knowledge, and resources. With this insight and experience, Ms. Knight created WEC to empower professional women across the nation and beyond.

Outside of WEC, Ms. Knight has extensive experience serving on boards and dedicating her expertise to a wide range of organizations:

- Presented to Kaufmann Foundation FastTrac entrepreneurs, Big 4 accounting firms, SBC (now AT&T) Professional Women's Group, and Physicians via University Endowment
- One of the first sponsors of Mid-America Angels Association
- Served as a Chamber Champion for the Kansas City Chamber of Commerce
- Council Member of the Economic Development Council in Leawood, Kansas
- Member of Rotary Club of Overland Park, Kansas
- Church Trustee and volunteer
- Board Member of the Truman Medical Center Charitable Foundation, American Lung Association, and HOA

Deborah Knight, J.D.
Women's Executive Club, LLC
11936 W. 119th St. #104
Overland Park, KS 66213
913-449-4996
president@WomensEC.com
www.WomensEC.com

Renee Raville

Following Your True North

Even as a little girl, I was a spiritual person. Being raised in a Catholic household when I was in elementary school, I was taught to pray to the saints and ask different angels for help. I remember deciding in the first grade that all of this seemed very complicated and was a lot to remember. I preferred going directly to the source. I was a precocious child. So, when I would say my prayers, they would all usually start out about the same, "Okay God, I know I am supposed to pray to a saint but I don't remember which one and I would just rather talk with you, so please don't be mad at me and please listen." Then I would say whatever I had to say and voice the concerns that a girl in the first or second grade has. As charming as this memory is, it laid a framework at an early age for spiritual connection. It was the belief in something bigger than myself, and an appreciation for ritual and ceremony, to a modest degree. I kept it interesting and would also pray and sing in the bushes while playing in the dirt in the backyard and doing the weird things that kids do. There is no rhyme or reason. I remember those days rather fondly and whimsically. It was so freeing to not need a logical reason behind everything that I did. When questioned about doing something wrong or bothersome, my consistent answer was, "I don't know", much to my parents' chagrin. I needed to have reasons behind why I did what I did. It needed to make sense. There needed to be orderly logic and planning behind it. This is complicated when you are in the second or third grade. *It seemed like a good idea at the time* was clearly not going to cut it in my household. It was also made very clear to me that logic and reason reigned over feelings. Feelings were subordinate to reason. Feelings needed to make sense or be ignored. Certainly, as an adult, I understand the need for this, to an extent. I just can't help but feel that by subordinating one way of being over the other, we lose something in the process. We subordinate our feelings and our bodies, to a large degree since we use our bodies to feel with, in favor of logic and reason—the mind. We become disconnected, if not downright uncomfortable in our bodies—in our own skin.

I remember being labeled as *overly sensitive* by my father. I have kept this label. However, now as I write this I must ask myself, what does this even mean? Was it simply that I was a little girl that was in touch with my feelings, had a lot of them, expressed them openly, and expressed them to a man that was a first time father, only child, and grew up in a reportedly cold, strict, and structured environment? Perhaps. It is interesting to consider the labels that we have placed upon us, and in turn place upon others, and don't think about what they really mean or what we are really saying when we wield our words. After all, we define ourselves by various labels and categories. You would think we would be more cautious when we dole these labels out. I don't think that we are. I know that I still struggle with this, especially when I am angry. Many times I come crawling back to the person I fought with, tail between my legs, and owe them a heartfelt apology. It is not always easy. I try to do this often. I'm imperfectly human but that was how we were built. Or is it? Maybe being perfectly human is being able to accept our humanity and its seemingly imperfect aspects, for what they are. It is nothing more and nothing less. Maybe this would be easier without all of these labels. I don't know for sure. I know that I am trying to be careful with the labels and words I wield these days and just when I think I am making radiant strides of progress, someone comes into my life that challenges them to their core. It makes me realize that I have a lot of work to do. I recently received a magnet from my aunt for my refrigerator that is a quote from Sai Baba saying, "Before you speak, ask yourself, is it kind? Is it necessary? Is it true? Does it improve upon the silence?"

When I was in middle school, my family moved from East Detroit to Lapeer, Michigan. I was starting the fifth grade. Entering a new school system was scary, awkward, and challenging. Nonetheless, I was resilient and adjusted relatively quickly. Our family went through a significant change as well. We started attending a community church in the local town. Apparently, there wasn't a Catholic church nearby. The community church was a *born again* church. My family converted to being *born again,* and became friends with some of the parishioners that were starting to go to yet a different local church, that was even more eccentric than this one. At the new church, many parents homeschooled their children. They really did not believe it was okay to listen to secular music. They also thought that you were supposed to spend your time with people of like-minded faith so as to not get the world's poison mixed into their pure system. As I write this, I am trying hard to not say snippy sarcastic comments or blatantly express my disdain. I begrudge no one their beliefs. I myself am a very spiritual person to this day, in my own way. However, I watched my family change and judgment skyrocketed. I understand that many people of faith insist this is not the way this belief system is supposed to be and I am relieved to hear that. Again, I am not knocking anyone's faith but merely sharing my experience.

I have journaled since I was about 12 years old. It was only a year or two ago, that I went back and finally opened them up and read them. I am 35 now. I have carried them with me this whole time. I couldn't open them but they were a core part of my experience. They validated my experiences, and my feelings. There is not enough room here to digress into all the details of the changes that this religious conversion brought about. That is for an entire book. However, I can recap the highlights. My brother, sister, and I were pulled out of public school and homeschooled for religious reasons. Let me stop here and quickly address the topic of homeschooling. I have nothing against it and realize that it is becoming more common, especially in Chicago. This makes sense when you learn about all of the budget cuts in the education system. I simply think it needs to be done with thought and care. The social aspect needs to be addressed and replaced constructively. We were homeschooled and my parents both worked full time. I was the oldest and we had farm animals (rabbits, chickens, geese, a horse, and a couple dogs). This meant that there were many days where I spent my time doing chores, doing my school work, trying to help my brother and sister with school work, and feeling left out and wondering what I was missing with my peers. Since spending time with nonbelievers was looked down upon, I was met with a fair amount of criticism at times for wanting to spend time with my school friends. That was, when they remembered to spend time with me, and to their credit they were pretty good about it. However, I still always felt like I was the odd one out and as though I was missing out. In fact, to this day, I hate feeling like I am missing out on stuff. I was 14 at this time. I felt like the more I read my Bible and the better Christian I became, the tighter the reigns were getting on me. I felt stuck and trapped. I started getting in trouble and rebelling. Actually, that is an understatement. I totally flipped out when I was 14. I was in a blind rage towards my father and family as a whole. I decided that if I was going to get in trouble for doing things like reading my Bible before I got my chores done; I was about to do some stuff that was actually worth getting in trouble for! I was very successful at this new goal. It entailed many nights sneaking out, running away with a girlfriend to New York, dying my hair every color of the rainbow, and being met with increasingly severe punishments. We were fueling one another's fire. I felt like I was losing all of my oxygen. I started having my anti-Christian clothing and other belongings burned. Things became really intense and unsafe. I left home a second time, determined not to return. I didn't.

I lived with my aunt and uncle for one or two years, until I was old enough to get emancipated. I will never forget how awful it was to announce to my aunt that I was doing this. I read my journal entries from that time period and still cringe. It is amazing how our minds can forget facts but our heart doesn't forget the feeling. I could not acknowledge at the time how big and scary this decision was. It was only upon reflection of these events in my 30s, that my heart bled and I wept for myself—for the little girl going through those things seemingly alone—full of rage and fear but also full of fire, hope, and dreams unformed but unapologetically present. Emancipation had actually been my plan since I learned about it at 14 years old. Legally, you needed to be 16 to apply for emancipation. You then talk to a judge and an attorney. You have to be living on your own before the actual court date where you plead your case and a judge determines if you are granted the emancipation and remain on your own or if you have to return home. I prepared for this process and saved money from the jobs that I worked between 14 and 16 years of age. I created a budget. I made plans. I adjusted the plans as I learned more information and gathered more facts. Even though my aunt and uncle provided a lovely home for me, I never wavered from that goal of emancipation. I did not feel that I could rest securely until I created my own safe space and home in the world. I did.

The following several years were met with a myriad of colorful challenges. They included employment choices, bad decisions in relationships, and struggling to work full time while getting my high school diploma. Ironically, I homeschooled myself with the assistance of a *correspondence program* to officially keep track of my records. I then enrolled and put myself through college. I had no idea what I was doing and made many mistakes along the way. I did it anyway.

School had become my source of structure and stability. There were deadlines, rules, expectations, and consistency. School became a sort of surrogate parent. I decided to major in psychology because I decided it would be cheaper to get a degree in psychology than pay for all the counseling I probably needed. I shared this with my counselor. He laughed. However, he did not disagree. I knew that I would need a graduate degree to do the work I wanted in this field. I made it happen.

At first, my grades were a struggle due to lifestyle choices. I made the necessary changes. A four-year relationship then ended in flames, and by *flames* I mean I realized my partner was totally leading a double life. It was like the kind that you read about in novels or pop culture magazines. School became my focal point to get me through a very long period of time where whenever I looked at myself in the mirror, I thought, "Yep, this is happening. This is your freaking life." I applied for a couple of scholarships. One was for minorities. I am Caucasian. I reasoned that I was a minority by virtue of being emancipated. My whole situation was unique. To my amazement, they agreed. I received the scholarship/fellowship and this placed me on a PhD track. I even graduated with numerous sets of honors. I then applied to graduate schools, certain that with these great achievements I would be accepted into my top choices. I was rejected by every school where I'd applied. I would have to wait an entire year to reapply. I decided to spend that year living in a different state. I had certainly traveled to different states and countries but only ever lived in Michigan. After I did this, I applied that following year to a single program that I found, researched, and knew was perfect for me. I was accepted.

I refused to let my circumstances dictate my lot in life. I refused to settle. I wanted to do amazing things. I had hopes, dreams and goals. I refused to let anything break those. Hope was the torch that lit my path. I have learned that it is a universal torch that keeps everyone going. Everyone needs hope. This was confirmed by my clients when I was doing case management work in Chicago. Hope is universally necessary, much like love, for our growth, healing, and overall existence. If we don't have something to believe in, then why bother? Hope is the belief in something larger than ourselves. I am grateful to my family for instilling me with that core foundational belief at a young age. Once I got older and figured out my own spiritual path, it served me quite well.

Where is this all leading and what is my point? What is *remarkable?* People tend to think remarkable refers to those big moments where something huge happens. I think what is remarkable is our ability to persevere and maintain momentum during all those unremarkable moments that tie the big experiences together. I know that in many of my unremarkable moments – day to day life—it can be a struggle to shower and show up for a job you don't really like. Sometimes that is as *remarkable* as things get. I find it remarkable how similar I am to the little girl that started journaling when she was 12 years old. I still have the same insecurities. They're just dressed in different clothing.

I still have this pervasive sense of anxiety about life in general. It has lessened over the years, but it still exists. I still have this hope that I can do something to help others, along with myself, feel comfortable in their own skin. To feel that we are enough just as we are. To simply *be* enough without succumbing to all the marketing out there that tells me that I have to be *this* or *that* or *have this* or *that* in order to be intelligent, successful, sexy and *enough.* I want to *intrinsically be* enough. I want to feel comfortable and secure in my own skin. After all, they say our bodies are a temple. They are certainly where we reside during our time on this earth. I have always wanted a space to call home. I have learned that no external dwelling will ever be safe or cozy enough until I am comfortable and whole within myself. *Being whole within ourselves,* for me, is the ultimate goal and the ongoing struggle. But I try. I will never give up. I will help others along the way to live a *simple life* with *simple health,* rooted in love and steeped in hope. I have created my line of plant based body care products as a vehicle to spread that message—conscious community that is seeking wholeness on every level, starting with themselves. This is how we make a change. This is how we start a revolution.

The word remarkable has French roots. *Remarquer* means, *to take note of.* Remarkable means taking note of what is going on within you and around you, having the courage to look at yourself in the mirror, create a safe and loving home within yourself, and share this experience with others so we all know that we are connected and not alone. We are all trying to get comfortable in our own skin. We all want a safe place to call home. We all yearn for simplicity. We all appreciate it when those around us can *take note* of their experiences and we relate to them. The journey for this wholeness can take us through dark places. It is usually darkness that we did not sign up for...or consciously remember signing up for. It usually has us screaming, "Why me!?" and throwing tantrums into a pillow so no one will hear us. It is not pretty. It is life. Life is messy. But it is real and if we *take note* of who we are through those experiences, we come through on the other side with a deeper appreciation for the sunshine. We realize that we have an inner strength and sparkle that we never noticed. We go within ourselves and deepen our sacred space and become more comfortable in our skin, knowing that we can persevere. We have done it before. We will do it again. We *take note* of what we learn. We cry about it to our friends. We realize the wholeness in asking for help or a sympathetic ear. We *take note* and bear witness to and for ourselves. This is where it starts—within our own skin. This will build a conscious community that is rooted in *enough-ism* and secure within themselves. This is how we are all remarkable as both individuals and as a community.

Renee Raville

Renee Raville is an educator, bodyworker, and the owner/creator of Simple Life. Simple Health. She creates and sells her own line of all natural plant based body care products to provide a slice of homemade healing for the soul that connects urban dwellers with Mother Nature. She has a Master's Degree in Holistic Psychology, attended a Master's program for Traditional Chinese Medicine, and has certifications in Massage Therapy, Reiki, Aromatherapy, and Herbalism. She passionately expresses her heart and soul through her customized bodywork sessions known as Soma Gnosis™ to help other creatives move past their blocks. Every item created in her product line is infused with her soulful intention to bring love, balance, and peace to the universal community. She speaks and educates academically and motivationally. In addition to building her business and practice, she actively works in the community and is compiling her journals and memoirs into a book project where she talks about her crazy life experiences, pontificates about the silver lining for everything that has happened, and uses her experiences to connect with others in a meaningful way. Check out her personal website at reneeraville.com to learn more about her business, book, practice, and projects.

Renee Raville
Simple Life. Simple Health.
312-869-0726
773-717-6290
reneeraville@simplelifesimplehealth.com
www.reneeraville.com

Nicole Michelle

Transformational Journey

We, the willing, led by the all-knowing
Are doing the impossible for the ungrateful.
We have done so much for so long with so little;
We are now capable of doing anything with absolutely nothing.
We are fearless, transformational leaders.

I have learned that none of us are born winners or losers, but we are all born choosers. Our lives become the culmination of the choices and decisions that we make. With that being said, victory has been my only option and I have always made a conscious decision to succeed no matter what adversities or obstacles have crossed my path. Graduating as the valedictorian from Dillard University in 1996 was my purposeful vindication for being denied my high school class rank as salutatorian. I became the first paternal and maternal grandchild to matriculate at a four-year college or university.

Upon graduation from college, I joined Price Waterhouse, LLP, which was one of the "Big 6" international accounting firms at that time. Although I was actively courted by five of the Big 6 firms, I decided to join Price Waterhouse because of their blue chip client base in the energy capital of the world, Houston, Texas. I started my career in the Assurance and Business Advisory Services Practice as an Audit Associate in the energy line of the business. My primary clients were ExxonMobil Corporation and Shell Oil Company. These high profile clients afforded me numerous opportunities to work on financial statement audit projects, defined benefit and defined contribution plan audits, multi-million dollar carve out transactions and other specialized projects.

I garnered the highly coveted designation as a Certified Public Accountant in the State of Texas in October 1997. In July 1998, I was promoted to Senior Associate. I was well-positioned in the firm with the potential to reach partner status within 10 years. However, I had lost my enthusiasm and interest for working in the energy industry. At that time, I did not have a professional mentor nor did I have a full understanding of the importance of building a personal brand and professional network.

I was approached by one of my sorority sisters, who was the Associate Director of the Human Resources Department at a competitor, to become a Supervising Senior Audit Associate in the Assurance and Advisory Business Services Practice in the healthcare line of the business. Without any guidance or career consultation, I joined the Houston Office of Ernst & Young, LLP, another "Big 5" accounting firm at that time, in February 1999. Ernst & Young had more than 50 percent of the audit market share for healthcare organizations in Houston. My client base included some of the largest hospital systems in the United States.

I rationalized my decision to join Ernst & Young by the slight career advancement, a 25 percent pay increase and an opportunity to enhance my resume with another major accounting firm and a second industry expertise in healthcare. What I did not realize was that the 25 percent pay increase I initially received, would quickly become diluted by the nominal four percent raise I would receive in the subsequent year. I also learned that being an Audit Associate was primarily the same at all of the "Big 5" accounting firms. The only difference was the brand name in which you worked. In November 2000, I began to reflect on my short-term career at both firms, my boredom in the audit practices and what would be a fulfilling career to me as a CPA.

One Sunday night, I began to pray and do some intensive soul searching. I thought about the special projects that I had executed at both firms. The most fulfilling and rewarding projects that I had worked on were related to mergers and acquisitions. I immediately had an epiphany. I discovered that I wanted to work on transactions in the mergers and acquisitions practice. I created an account on Monster.com and began to perform a search for career opportunities in transactions. I applied for opportunities to become a Senior Associate in Transaction Practices with Arthur Andersen, LLP and KPMG, LLP. I received call backs and interviews from both firms. As destiny would have it, I received the best offer and a 35 percent pay increase from the Houston office of KPMG, LLP.

In November 2000, I launched my new career at KPMG and met the man who would later become my husband. This is when my transformational journey began. Little did I know that I would climb the corporate ladder and spiral down in the abyss of love. Similar to many others, I wanted to live the American dream.

I started my career in Transaction Services and worked there for eight years. I was able to achieve the ranks of Manager and Director while I was there.

With the start of my newfound career in mergers and acquisitions, I realized that something was missing. I did not have anyone to share my career success with and to enjoy the finer luxuries that life had afforded me. I had been working in the largest accounting firms in the world, sometimes 70 or 80 hours a week. I had been a bridesmaid multiple times but never a bride. Would I ever find love? Would love ever find me? Would I be another female corporate success who would have to sacrifice her personal life and family for a career? For the first time, I believed that I understood what it meant when people said, "it is lonely at the top." One thing I knew for sure, I did not want to be alone. I wanted to have it all, including a successful career and loving marriage. In March 2002, I got married.

My career continued to flourish. In July 2002, I was promoted to a Transaction Services Manager. I was the only female in the entire Southwest

Region in the practice at that time working with 14 Anglo males. I gained valuable experience in working with corporate executives, investment bankers and high-powered law firms. I met with, prepared presentations and presented to corporate boards and audit committees. I worked on multiple transactions that ranged in deal sizes from $100.0 million to $40.0 billion. I worked on cross-border transactions with Canada, China, Germany, Japan, Mexico, Spain and the UK.

After a year of marriage, my husband and I decided that we wanted to start a family. That same year, I was medically diagnosed as infertile. Upon hearing the news, I felt like my world was being shattered. At that point in my life, I wanted nothing more than to have a child. In January 2004, I began my fertility treatments. With much fasting and prayer, I became pregnant in April 2004. I remember the joy and excitement that I felt. While my family and I were elated, the announcement of the news at work was met with considerable pessimism. The truth of the matter was that there were very few women who worked in the Transaction Services Practice in the entire firm nationwide and there was not one working mother in the entire practice.

In July 2004, the practice held its national training meeting in Florida. While I was there, I noticed each dialogue that I had with the various partners and management team members of the practice had the same underlying tone— my career trajectory and choice would likely change due to the high demands of a career in the transactions space and the fact that the role had never been attempted to be executed or entertained by a working mother. On the flight back to Houston, I made a pivotal decision, I decided that I wanted to and would become the first working mother in the entire Transaction Services Practice at KPMG USA. I had no idea of the personal and professional obstacles that I would encounter on my journey to that destination.

In January 2005, my daughter was born and I experienced a severe battle with post-partum depression. It caused me to be hospitalized for more than three weeks. My recovery was difficult and caused me to be disconnected professionally while I was on maternity leave. The environment in which I worked had a silent code that required me to check in with the office while I was on maternity leave. My limited interaction with the office while I was on maternity leave, left my partners wondering if I was going to still have "my head in the game" and be fully engaged and dedicated when I returned to work.

At the end of May 2005, I returned to work with very limited time to prove that I was ready for promotion to Director. At the end of September 2005, my partner informed me that I would not get my expected promotion to Director in October 2005. I would have to prove to the firm that I could be a successful working mother and maintain my standard of excellent performance one more year before being considered for promotion to Director the following year.

At that moment of disappointment, I had a choice to make. I could either become angry and upset or I could choose to be victorious. I chose the latter. At that time, I decided to change career counselors. My request was granted. I met with my new career counselor at the beginning of the new fiscal year. We had a courageous conversation about my career. We discussed all of the opportunities that could and would be made available to me. The outcome of the conversation was that the firm would be committed to me as long as I demonstrated my commitment to the firm with excellent performance. My maternal grandmother agreed to care for my new baby when I returned to work. She would come to our home every weekday morning and stay at my home overnight when I traveled for business. I was determined to brand myself as a "Superwoman" and demonstrate that a woman could have it all—career success as well as being a working wife and mother. I decided that I would do whatever it took to make it to the next level in my career. That fiscal year was one of the most amazing years in my professional career.

From a personal standpoint, my marriage was failing and quickly unraveling. I had many public successes and even more private failures. The perception of many was "Little House on the Prairie" but my reality was

"Nightmare on Elm Street." No one knew, personally or professionally, that I was in an emotionally, mentally and verbally abusive marriage. When my husband became abusive, I decided to become more consumed with my career and professional success. I had somehow convinced myself that my career success would alleviate my personal pain. Over time, I learned to lead a double life. My peak performance at work compensated for my failing marriage.

In October 2006, I was promoted to Transaction Services Director. My promotion garnered me numerous rewards and recognition. I became an advocate and champion for work-life effectiveness. Work life balance is virtually non-existent. You do what you have to do at home and you do even more at work. Your attitude, work ethic and philosophy determine your work-life effectiveness. When client demands diminish or subside, you learn to take advantage of the downtime but you are always connected professionally. During my career, I never took a vacation that was for rest and relaxation. All of my vacations were working days off. My vacation tours and excursions would be scheduled around client teleconference calls and reporting deadlines, regardless of whether my vacation destination was domestic or international. I had become accustomed to doing whatever it took to get my job done in excellence. I thrived on being able to meet and exceed client expectations. My greatest satisfaction would come from getting a complimentary email from a client thanking me for a job well done, the extensive hours worked, and for going above and beyond the call of duty.

My corporate responsibility, volunteerism initiatives and programs, impeccable work ethic and performance as a working mother afforded me opportunities to mentor hundreds of women on work-life effectiveness. In 2006, I was awarded the Chairman's Award for the Houston Business Unit for my excellence and achievements in community service and philanthropic activities. I served as the Mentoring Chairperson for the Houston Diversity Council. I was appointed to the Transaction Services Organizational Development Task Force where we were challenged with identifying challenges and implementing solutions that would reduce practice turnover, improve project performance, appropriately retain and reward employees and create an improved working environment for all of the practice professionals. I was also appointed to the Women's Advisory Board, the national council for KNOW (KPMG Network of Women.)

My career continued to soar while my marriage continued to decline. In September 2008, Lehman Brothers collapsed and the mergers and acquisitions market became very uncertain and even halted in certain instances. My two largest clients suspended their acquisition programs and my managed revenue and productivity quickly diminished. In November 2008, I was included in a reduction in force that resulted in being laid off from KPMG. My successful eight-year career had concluded.

After my layoff, the emotional, mental and verbal abuse from my husband became more intense. Unfortunately for me, I could not camouflage my pain with career success.

In 2009, I launched Madison Brothers Consulting Group, a specialized tax consulting and business advisory services practice. My certification as a CPA, professional experience and prior client base that included Fortune 1000 companies in the oil and gas, power, oilfield services, healthcare, technology, real estate, business services and manufacturing and distribution industries afforded me opportunities to continue to consult and advise various business entities and organizations.

In 2011, I accepted my spiritual call into ministry despite the lack of support from my husband. Within months, I decided to discontinue my double life and I left my husband. I no longer wanted to live a public dream and a private nightmare.

Since that time, an entire new world opened up for me. Madison Brothers Consulting Group now has an affiliation with a tax consulting firm that has secured more than $350 million in tax incentives for various corporations across multiple industries. I am also a Certified Coach, Speaker and Trainer with The John Maxwell Team.

My path and experiences have allowed me to serve Fortune 1000 companies, Russell 2000 companies, not-for-profit organizations, corporate executives and leadership teams. From a business consulting prospective, our firm's focus is the success of our clients. We are able to identify strategies to enhance revenue, improve profitability, reduce expenses and optimize employee performance. From a coaching and leadership prospective, I facilitate lunch and learn sessions, seminars, workshops and mastermind groups that train individuals, executives, leadership teams and organizations to develop, execute and implement strategies and solutions that produce the desired outcomes that are mutually beneficial to the individuals, leaders, teams and the people who employ them, partner with them, work with them and serve with them.

Challenges are opportunities to improve people, processes and profits.

From a spiritual, professional and personal perspective, I have learned that authenticity is the greatest liberator. If you do not know who you are, you cannot determine where you are going. Image and status were priorities in my twenties. As I have transformed over the years, the most important thing to me is TRUTH. Learning to be honest with yourself and being released from the pressures and facades of society allow you to exhale from a lifestyle that can easily suffocate you.

I wore different faces in various places. I have been able to remove the mask at home; at church; at civic and community meetings; in the business community and in the MIRROR. I used to look at myself in the mirror and imagine what I wanted to see just to be a "pretender" each and every day. Now, I can look in the mirror and see a beautiful woman who has been fearfully and wonderfully made. My story has and will change many others.

My life's purpose is to leave a handprint and footprint on every individual, leader, executive, business or organization that I encounter. Handprints touch the heart and empower the mind, body, soul and spirit. Footprints blaze the trail and the path that everyone must walk to guide them into their unique destiny.

Nicole Michelle

Nicole Michelle is a woman of prayer and power. She is a multi-talented, Proverbial 31 Woman of God who firmly believes that when much is given, even more is required. Nicole is very active in her local business, church and civic community. She is a mother, mentor, executive business woman, humanitarian, philanthropist, publisher and Independently Certified Speaker, Coach and Teacher with the John Maxwell Team. Nicole Michelle is also a Certified Public Accountant who has almost 20 years of experience in accounting, business consulting, financial advisory services, internal and external financial auditing, mergers and acquisitions, project management and tax consulting.

Her clients include Fortune 500 clients in the oil and gas, power, oilfield services, healthcare, professional services, business services, banking, and technology industries.

She also enjoys serving portfolio companies of private equity firms, start-ups and not-for-profit organizations.

She believes that no one is born a winner or loser, but we are all born choosers. SUCCESS is the only option.

Nicole Michelle
Madison Brothers Consulting Group
3200 Southwest Freeway, Suite 3300
Houston, TX 77027
832-264-8668
mynameisvictory74@gmail.com
www.NicoleMichelleCoaches.com

Sarah Gleeson

The Power of Permission

The uncertainty of what was to become of my life brewed a fear within me that became completely consuming. I found myself weeping and isolated as I began to surrender to the idea that my life was not turning out the way I had wanted it to. I could not have foreseen the circumstances that led me to this chaotic existence but never the less I was in it. I had to decide quickly what my options were and what I was going to do next.

The trouble had started for me a few years earlier. I had always imagined that when I grew up and began to live my life it would be that "happily ever after" kind. Not once had I considered that I would be continuously disappointed and struggle with it. I know that success and happiness is never guaranteed but I always did the right things in the attempt of getting the right results. It just never worked out that way for me. Everything I seemed to do back-fired and instead of moving forward, I was always falling behind. When things got complicated, I would either resist it or conjure up creative ways to deal with it. The more I tried to fix what wasn't working in my life, the more my life seemed to turn to crap. I would often say "if only I could get from where I am to where I want to be." The truth was that I didn't have a clue what the hell I needed to do differently. I felt completely lost and alone. I had spent so many years doing what everyone suggested I do, that when an opportunity presented itself for me to make a decision for myself, I resisted it with full force. I struggled to abandon the belief that everything I tried would result in another failure. I trusted nothing and no one—not even myself sometimes. The faith needed to believe that change was possible was a deep reach and it didn't come easily.

Almost immediately after I got married to my husband, I began to have doubts about whether or not I should have gone through with it. We had a young child together already and I was torn between whether to build her a family or break it apart. My husband and I had very different ideas about spirituality, parenting and money. There are thousands of experts in the world preaching that even one of these differences in a relationship can doom it. However, I had made the decision not to listen to their wisdom and to continue with what I thought I should do for the sake of my daughter's future and stability. Everything I had learned about marriage growing up, told me that you stick to it no matter what. I had confided in a few trusted friends about my doubts and yet every one of them told me I was having "cold feet" and my feelings were a natural part of getting married. I intuitively disagreed. Unfortunately, I felt at that time that I didn't have a choice. I felt that if I didn't follow through on this commitment that the outcome would have long term repercussions with a cost that I was not prepared to pay.

My marriage only survived a couple of years. Had I been confident in trusting my instincts and feelings, I'm positive the course of my relationship would have changed. It would most likely have still ended at some point because we were so incredibly different. Yet, in the moment of ending what we did have, the facts didn't seem to matter. I found myself trying to make sense of our marriage and tried to understand why I had made the choices that I did. All I could think about was how right I was in not trusting him. In the little time that we were husband and wife, he had created a path of destruction that literally devastated and destroyed me. I was a single mother and I was broken.

When I moved out of the house I had with my husband, I left him everything. I only took my clothes, my daughter's clothes and her bed. I was starting from nothing and I was terrified. The greatest loss was not that the relationship had ended but that I had lost myself in the process. I suffered in silence as everyone around me experienced what their hearts had desired. I did not have a positive attitude or optimistic outlook for the future. I believed that my daughter's happiness was more important than mine so I continued to make bad choices. I learned not to dream or wish. I had taught myself to have the expectation that nothing good was ever going to happen for me and for a very long time I fulfilled my own prophecy.

Not long after the divorce, I had to file for bankruptcy. I guess the struggle to get by wasn't enough of a challenge because now I was struggling to literally survive. I had lost my job and there was no money coming in but there was a whole lot of it needing to go out. I had been threatened with eviction by my landlord but I simply didn't have the money I owed him. The day I discovered the meaning of "shame", was the day that I lined up for three hours in front of the government office to apply for emergency Public Housing. I was astonished at the lack of compassion and the obvious distain from those there who were supposed to be helping me. It had taken me three weeks to pack away my pride and go there in the first place. I couldn't believe how horrible it felt to be judged for my misfortunes. I wasn't there because I was too lazy to get a job or spent my money on frivolous things. Even if I had been there because of other circumstances, it still wouldn't have justified the attitude and intolerance I received from my so called "helpers". I was in this financial position because I had escaped a bad marriage. I now understood why it was so hard for so many people to get back on track when things went wrong. I had just assumed that the world would have compassion for someone like me but I had been wrong. I learned through this experience that as determined as I was to change my circumstances, the system that was supposed to help me was stacked against me. This awareness created an enormous passion in me to help others—I just hadn't realized it yet.

It took me four more years to find my way out of the mess. I eventually did receive a place to live through public housing. I had found a job that gave me the financial potential to turn things around for us. It was still a massive struggle to make ends meet because I owed everyone money. Creditors and financial threats happened on a daily basis. However, I could afford my rent, my daughter's needs were being met and I was beginning to believe in hope for the future once again.

It was around this time that I began to consider the idea of stepping into the dating arena. It wasn't that I was looking for Mr. Right. In fact, the idea of a relationship and the process to build one was quite terrifying for me. I decided to try. Under no circumstances did I reveal my financial status or discuss the weight of the baggage I carried. As a result, the men that I met through dating did not turn into any lasting relationships. On the surface, I was totally okay with being alone but inside I was yearning for love. It had been such a long time since I'd felt it and I desperately wanted to feel it again.

Anyone who understands the Laws of Attraction knows that what you think about, you bring about. I had just spent years fighting poverty, judgements, disappointments and trauma. There hadn't been many examples of me thinking about what was possible and thinking optimistically. Therefore, as I continued to date, it shouldn't be any surprise that the men I was attracting weren't the Prince Charming's I had hoped for. I continued to choose men who replicated what I had experienced before. Men who lied and took advantage of me seemed to be a consistent theme. It was emotionally and psychologically exhausting. I really began to believe that there was something wrong with me. Was it a karmic payback? I couldn't think of what I had done to deserve this type of struggle and disappointment but it seemed to surround me. I was so tired of nothing being easy!

Then one day I met a man who, for a brief moment in time, made me believe that my luck had changed. He was smart, wealthy and ambitious. When we first, met our time together was amazing and I was simply smitten with everything about him. Yet, as the weeks progressed, I began to discover a different side of him. It didn't take long for me to realize that he wasn't going to be my champion. Truth be told, he became the most emotionally and spiritually destructive man I had ever known. Unfortunately, the additional problem that came from dating this man was that I ended up pregnant. As if my history with making choices hadn't already provided me enough to struggle with, I was now adding this problem to the equation. The father and I did not stay together. Therefore, I now found myself as a single parent for the second time.

I was devastated and immediately went into panic mode about the struggle that awaited me. I was so angry with myself. I had been working so hard to improve my situation and now all that I had done were simply meaningless efforts. How was I going to tell my daughter that I was pregnant? Her whole life had been dictated to her because of my struggles. And yet again, she would be directly and negatively impacted by my inability to provide for her. I felt trapped. I felt like there was nothing that could have possibly been worse to deal with. I had just spent fourteen years trying to overcome the obstacles my marriage had created and now, in one event, I found myself back at square one with desperation and a lack of hope. Nothing worse was possible than to discover I was pregnant. However, it would have been impossible for me to predict at that time that the worse was still to come.

I remember clearly the day I felt a strange twinge in my belly. Nothing had happened but it was a feeling that I'll never forget because I "knew" that something was wrong. I was five months pregnant and up until then all had been well. My doctor had known me for years and had learned to respect my intuitive reasons for visiting him without asking me too many questions. It was a Friday afternoon at three o'clock. He told me that he would see if I could be scheduled for an ultrasound as soon as possible. I managed to get an appointment for four o'clock that same day. When I arrived at the radiology center, the receptionist informed me that their center would be closing in about half an hour and I was fortunate that the sonographer agreed to book the appointment. Two hours later, well after the clinic was supposed to have closed, I was told that my baby's heart looked a bit large but that I shouldn't be too alarmed. She told me that she would forward the results to the doctor but because it was the weekend, I shouldn't expect to hear back until Monday. It was now six o'clock and the radiology center and my doctor's clinic were both closed.

I hadn't made it home yet when my cellphone rang. It was my doctor. He was calling to ask if I could come in and see him in the morning. He told me that he needed to go over the ultrasound notes and could make room for me a half hour before he was booked to see his first patient. I was suspicious about the calm statements I had received to this point, because of how eager he was now to see me.

The next morning, I was told that my baby had an enlarged heart. He tried to ease my concern by telling me that I would be getting an appointment at the hospital perinatology department so that they could do additional tests. He insisted I didn't need to be overly concerned and that I shouldn't expect this appointment to happen for several weeks. There was so much going on that was out of my control. I received a call on Monday at eight a.m. from the hospital asking if I could be there at nine. I knew immediately that this was not going to be good.

I arrived at the appointment and was brought promptly into the exam room. Within moments of the exam beginning, the room turned silent. After ninety minutes, I demanded to know what was going on. The radiologist came in and everyone else took his cue and left the room. I was told that my baby was doing very well in utero but that there was a significant problem with her heart. Her heart lacked the interior construction and did not have the capability to work properly. It was explained that my daughter was probably going to die from heart failure upon birth. He compassionately began to tell me about the complications both on the interior and the exterior of her heart. The doctor explained that I would have to make some difficult choices immediately.

This was my "rock bottom" moment. The real problem that took me forever to admit until then was that I had always focused on what was wrong with me or wrong in my life. Listening to the doctor tell me that I was literally in a life or death battle for my baby who had done nothing wrong to deserve this struggle, gave me the "a-ha" moment that changed everything! I saw for the very first time in my life that I had never given myself the permission I needed to have my own thoughts, my own feelings or my own desires. I had always done what people suggested I do or done things that I felt I had to do.

What became clear to me was that I had lived my entire life as a victim. Everything always happened to me. It was far easier to be a victim in life than to take on the responsibility for my thoughts and actions. It took this experience to realize that the stories I had been telling myself over and over again for years were excuses. Each time that I did not use my voice and did what everybody else wanted me to do, there was only one thing happening – I was sabotaging myself. I realized that I had never allowed myself to dream big or want big. It hit me like a ton of bricks that what I had always done was ignore my personal desires and wants.

Had I been told that giving myself permission to do what I wanted to do could change my reality, I would never have believed it. I realized that the power I felt when I gave myself permission to do what I wanted to do, opened doors and created opportunities that I had previously been blind to. I was beginning to understand that it wasn't the events or circumstances in my life that were dictating my potential. It was me. I was learning that I hadn't been giving myself permission to do my own thing because I didn't want to offend someone else. It never even occurred to me that every time I denied myself my wants and needs, it was I that was being offended.

So often we try to make justified choices and it often results in our making the wrong ones. I had been a victim in life for so long I had lost sight of what I was capable of. It had been easier to complain and blame others when things didn't work out as planned. We become so powerful when we give ourselves permission to move forward with our personal wants and needs. Giving ourselves permission, results in our ability to step into our personal power story on demand. It is one of the greatest things we can gift ourselves.

When we feel like we can create our life with the meaning and purpose that we design, we say "yes" way more often than we say "no". When we restrict ourselves from achieving our goals and dreams because we're limited by what we think we should do instead of what we could do, we are sabotaging our personal success and desires. The power in giving yourself permission provides you with the freedom to believe more, achieve more and receive more. Contrary to what you would expect, giving yourself permission to do what is in your best interest is not a selfish act. In fact, when you are consciously choosing what you do and do not want you will see more opportunities than obstacles. You will accomplish greater things than you could have previously imagined because your personal limitations are gone. Permission provides us an ongoing way to continuously grow and to be empowered.

Everyone will have their own unique experiences in life but what is common for all is that life is unpredictable. When everything goes according to plan, it's easy to step into your personal power and expand and explore your opportunities. When things are not going according to plan, then give yourself permission to expand and explore your opportunities anyway. Permission increases your ability to become the Remarkable Woman you were meant to be. You deserve to live the life you want to live instead of the life you have to live. Give yourself permission to live that life!

Sarah Gleeson

Sarah Gleeson has spent years inspiring her clients and audiences to get out of their comfort zones and get a front-row seat in life. After starting her career as a Certified Clinical Hypnotherapist and Mindset Coach, she is often affectionately referred to as the "Bullshit Buster" by her coaching clients and audiences. Sarah helps individuals and business owners that typically feel confined by their "Should's" and those that aspire to achieve greater results and say Yes way more than they do! Sarah's audiences and clients learn how to turn obstacles into opportunities. With her background in practical psychology, sales and her personal story of struggle and accomplishments, Sarah has honed her skills to reach people at their core beliefs and help them to realize their personal potential, personal possibilities and ultimately, their personal power story. With her engaging and fun personality, Sarah connects with her audiences immediately and delivers content that they can use right away.

In addition to being a popular motivational keynote speaker, Sarah is also the founder of the Mind Kanvas Institute and a Co-Founder of the worldwide transformational learning experience called "Bridges to Abundance".

When not delivering upbeat and motivational programs or coaching sessions, Sarah supports the Cardiac Units of the Stollery Children's Hospital for Sick Kids, The Alberta Children's Hospital and The Alzheimer's Society of Canada.

Sarah Gleeson
Sarah Gleeson
157 Windstone Park SW
Airdrie, Alberta T4B 4X5
403-478-3430
sarah@sarahgleeson.ca
www.sarahgleeson.ca

Jane Bishop

Will the Real YOU Please Stand Up?

In the movie *Martian Child,* Dennis is a six year old living his life under a box. He was abandoned by his parents, placed in a foster home, and socially rejected. He spent his days literally under a box with a small "window" cut out so he could see. To cope with being rejected and his circumstances, he convinced himself he was from Mars.

How many women experience life from under a box like Dennis? Many women have convinced themselves that they don't fit. This could be due to some label imposed by others, their own sense of inadequacy, or a lack of understanding of how they are gifted. The chosen coping skill is often to hide "under a box."

Consider the focus of this timely book: remarkable women. The very definition of *remarkable* gives many women an excuse to live life under a box. According to the Merriam Webster online dictionary, remarkable is defined as *"worthy of being or likely to be noticed especially as being uncommon or extraordinary."* Many women have created a self-limiting belief by convincing themselves they are anything but *uncommon or extraordinary* because they believe there is no headline to their story; no breaking news and no here's what's trending. In essence, some have become so immersed **living in their story** they cannot see life clearly and they have forgotten how to **stand on their story** for clarity, confidence and transformation.

When God created mankind, He instilled in us the desire for purpose. Finding our fit can be challenging, so why not simply live under one box to the next? In my experience, women often allow others to treat them like play dough, being molded and shaped to that person's image rather than God's image. It's uncomfortable, frustrating, and painful not to mention the tremendous energy drain to live a life that is not *you*. When we do that, we may be communicating to self we are not *remarkable;* i.e. giving up on being the person God created.

Growing up, I could have easily chosen to live my life under a box. I had the double whammy as some have said, of being a "PK (preacher's kid) and Army Brat." The first 18 years of my life, I moved with my family 18 times. That meant living in 11 cities, four states, and one foreign country. I experienced nine different schools including four different high schools. The longest we lived in one place was 35 months in Germany. It was not a question of "if we would move" but "when would we move?" I recall the day that my parents told my two brothers and me we were moving to Germany. As a 13-year-old whose worldview was not as expanded as it would become, I thought we had won a trip and would be taking an extended vacation! I innocently asked my Dad what we would do about school. He lovingly responded, "I guess you will go to school in Germany because we will live there for three years." Little did I know how my life was about to change.

Frequently being the new kid in town and school is only part of my story. In addition, I didn't wear the same style of clothes as other kids or participate in many of the activities my friends did. I remember being laughed at, called names, and not invited to be part of the "cool" crowd. I also had brown freckles, a large birthmark on my left leg, crooked teeth, a keloid scar on left arm, and as I got older, would choose not to drink or smoke. Compared to today's generation, all of that may seem minute. However, in the context of my time, it was as significant as the current day bullying—school age and adult—and other challenges that are trending.

I had a choice to make early in my life. I could allow other's expectations to determine how I should *fit* their image of my life, or choose to be content and fulfilled with how God made me, finding my *fit* through Him. Because of loving parents who believed in me, I chose to have confidence in the person that God had created, and learn to find my fit through Him. My parents continually reinforced my choice as they encouraged me to discover and be the person that God had created me to be. They taught me principles that I have used throughout my life as I **learned** how to live a consistent lifestyle of standing on my story.

It is important to notice the word **learned.** I did not wake up one morning and decide for the real me to stand up and it immediately or magically happened! In my archive files, are many examples of lessons learned as I was faced with the choice of living under a box or allowing the real me to stand up. None of them are "headliner" events. They are simply everyday life experiences that provide the opportunity to choose to stand on my story. Examples range from being left out to being discriminated against to being ridiculed and minimized in a workplace. At any point, the easy or default choice would have been to live under a box. However, if I had consistently taken that approach, I would have missed out on the adventure of being me!

One "opportunity" occurred during my junior year in college when two friends and I decided to go through an abbreviated process of pledging a sorority. This was an unexpected decision for me as I was not "into" the sorority life nor did I view myself as a "sorority girl" (whatever that means). We had a mutual friend who had gone through the full process and really raved about being part of the group, so we made the decision to "go for it." We passed all the tests including initiation (that's a funny story for another time) and were accepted.

All went well until half-way through my senior year. I related to all the sororities on campus as the student director for the women's intramural program. In that part-time paid position, I officiated many of the basketball and softball games when my sorority was not playing. I had been in this student director role since my freshman year and had many friends, regardless of what or if they were in a sorority. One of the foundational life lessons I learned growing up was to accept people as they are and make no judgments or distinction.

My approach of being friends with anyone regardless of their sorority affiliation was eventually perceived by my sorority sisters as being disloyal. They accused me of conspiring with the enemy (my interpretation) and basically had nothing to do with me the last few months of my senior year. I had been investing all that I had with a standard of excellence. I don't recall the details of why it all exploded. However, I do recall the day it exploded, what I felt and how I dealt with it. I was devastated, angry and hurt! When this happened, I left campus, went to my apartment, changed into running clothes and took off down the hill and onto "my" course. For five miles I sobbed, prayed, sobbed and prayed some more. At the end of the run, I acknowledged the crossroad. I was faced with the choice of the "living forward in spite of life" road by standing on my story and the "woe is me, how could they do this?" road. This was not the first time I found myself at such a crossroad and it would not be the last.

Perhaps you may be thinking *so what?* There is certainly nothing remarkable about your story. It is not extraordinary or uncommon. That may be true from your perspective. However, I invite you to keep reading.

Life is a journey full of cycles and sequences of activities. It is marked by events, moments, and opportunities. Some are unexpected and depleting; others are unexpected and invigorating. The journey requires fuel that recharges our internal batteries and feeds the soul, replenishes the body, refreshes the mind and nurtures the emotions. When our internal batteries get drained, the journey slows. As a result, the forward movement stalls and the default mode may be mediocrity. A limiting belief for many is "this is my story and is as good as it gets." Women are often so busy trying to *measure up,* that they have forgotten how *remarkable* they are and miss incredible experiences. I invite you to consider these questions:

- Where are you currently in life?

- How are you living forward?

- How are you consistently experiencing life as the real you?

- How does your current lifestyle reflect your attitude of life?

- What is it costing you for the real you *not* to stand up?

Training is Key

My choice of standing on my story so the real me can stand up consistently provides pathways for rewarding life experiences. My life has been enriched and my gifts and skills honed, as I have engaged my passion in four business environments: athletic, corporate, church and now as a solopreneur. Roles before being a solopreneur have included head women's basketball coach, assistant men's basketball coach, assistant dean of students/women, secretary, director of project development, worship planner/leader, soloist, curriculum developer, event planner, senior director, speaker and trainer. With each role, I was on the outer edge as I had been growing up. With each role came the opportunity to be mediocre or remarkable. With each role, there was the choice to live under a box or stand on my story. Mistakes have been made on the journey. Rejection, discrimination and isolation have been experienced. There were times when I was momentarily *living under a box.* It was frustrating, depleting and no fun. When I acknowledged I was at that place, I relied on my life training and did some "box busting" by allowing the real me to stand up! The release experienced was rewarding and replenishing!

When I was coaching basketball, practices were challenging by design. It was important for the athletes to train their physical and mental muscles so game performance would come naturally, especially when the muscle energy was depleted. This was clearly evident when our small college team played a college team out of our league. We were clearly the underdog. At the end of the game, we had been outplayed and outscored in every category except one —the final score. Because the athletes trusted their training, at the end of triple overtime we won! Wow!

Training is key in life as well. Once you train and practice standing on your story, the real you naturally stands up. Clarity and confidence exist consistently without thinking. The *remarkable* part is that any woman can stand on her story and experience her uncommon, extraordinary life! There is no one like you. You are unique, incredible, and awesome because *"God don't make no junk"* (Ethel Waters).

Box Busting

Although consistently confident in this life adventure, there are moments I am more comfortable "in my skin" than others. There are occasions when I momentarily resist stepping into my awesomeness. At times, I have a split second thought of self-doubt. However, because I have chosen to embrace how God has gifted me, I trust my life training and remain clear about who I am. I refuse to be "put in a box" by others and have participated in several "box busting" practices through the years.

Full disclosure: when you bust boxes, you don't fit in everyone's neat little package. As a result, people often don't quite know what to do with you. As I write this, many examples surface and evoke a smile. One I will share happened many years ago when I worked with a national organization that had a major conference in New Mexico every other year. One year, I was asked to emcee the evening sessions where over 2000 people were in attendance, including my parents. The "box busting" part came into play because I was female, unknown, and had no high ranking title/position. Each morning, my mother and I would go for a fitness walk. On the third morning walk, a lady stopped and asked, "Aren't you that person leading the evening sessions?" I answered yes. Then she asked, "Who are you, anyway?!" I politely answered and she went on her way. Mother and I burst out in laughter after she got out of hearing distance. I did not "fit" the concept of who would normally fill this role. Love it!

Back to the questions posed earlier. How did you answer? The real you standing up begins with what story you are telling yourself. Jim Loehr in the *The Power of Story* writes *"of all the stories we can read and/or tell, the most compelling story about storytelling is how we tell stories about ourselves."* Pause and think about that statement. If you did a quick fact check on the stories you tell about yourself, would the meter register false or true? Psychologist Justin Barrett adds, *"We automatically, and often unconsciously, look for an explanation of why things happen to us, and 'stuff just happens' is no explanation. Stories impose meaning on the chaos."* This may largely be due to the fact that our brain is wired to tell and understand stories.

Allow me to illustrate with a story. **Version one:** I am attending a conference and discover the color nail polish on one fingernail is about to peel off. I have no color polish with me, so I visit the hotel gift shop hoping they have a bottle of clear polish for repair. I find one bottle, purchase it and apply to the fingernail. "Catastrophe" is averted.

Version two: I am attending a conference and discover the color nail polish on one fingernail is about to peel off. I have no color polish with me, so I visit the hotel gift shop hoping they have a bottle of clear polish for repair. Thankfully, I find one bottle and take it to the register and hear it will be $9.62. At that moment, I have a decision to make. Pay the outlandish price and maintain my nail dignity or walk away and risk nail indignity. Of course, I purchased the bottle of clear polish! I ask you. Which version is more interesting? When I have shared that story, the immediate response is version two and generally evokes gasps and laughter from the group.

Our culture today thrives on headlines/what's trending more than ever before. We can thank technology for creating that climate. The plethora of data available online is somewhat daunting and people are creating new standards of how they think they must *measure up* and/or *keep up.* This may contribute to some being drawn unconsciously into the "imposter syndrome," a term coined in 1978 by clinical psychologists Pauline R. Clance and Suzanne A. Imes. It refers to high achievers who have so much self-doubt, that they are afraid of being exposed as a "fraud." Said differently, people consistently self-talk their way into self-doubt which leads to self-limiting beliefs which leads to _____—you fill in the blank. Think of a person you respect and admire who demonstrates how the real you stands up. What behavior do you observe? What language do you hear? How do you know they are standing **on** their story and not **in** their story? What do you learn from that person? How did they get to that point?

Your Story Unleashed

Another favorite movie is *Mr. Magorium's Wonder Emporium.* It is whimsical, mystical, and a fantasy. Mr. Magorium is an eternal optimist who owns a magical toy emporium. For most of the movie, he is trying to convince Mahoney that she is capable of taking over his magical toy emporium when he leaves. She consistently comes up with excuses. As the actors portray their roles, one of the main themes in the movie is clear: we all have unlimited potential that is waiting to be unleashed. Finally, when Mr. Magorium is about to depart, he takes Mahoney's face into his hands and claims, *"Your life is an occasion! Rise to it!"*

Willpower, alone, will not result in the real you standing up. According to David Bach, President of the Platypus Institute, each time we make a conscious decision (willpower), our unconscious mind is making 40,000 decisions. Do the math. The conscious decision is outnumbered 1:40,000! When a person desires to change a pattern, the unconscious behavior is identified and a plan is developed to interrupt the neural pathway. David Bach has proven that when we interrupt a neural pathway over and over for 30 days, the brain will be rewired and the old pathway resolved as if it never existed; i.e. we have to bust the "neural pathway box!"

So how can the real YOU please stand up? Delighted that you asked (I write with a smile on my face)! I am passionate about helping women stand on their story and step into their awesomeness. I don't know everything but what I know, I know well. Living4ward is the women's division of my business, Take The Next Step. The purpose is to provide resources for women to embrace their awesomeness around four essentials: reactivating passion, readjusting attitude, reapplying gifts and recapturing life. I offer **1:1 coaching plans** for individuals who make the *choice* for the real you to stand up. You may benefit from a foundation plan or from a refresher plan as you are strong in standing on your story. You may be a former "box buster" now living under a box and benefit from how to bust the box again plan. I invite you to visit www. takethenextstepcct.com and click on Living4ward or reach out to me by email, jane@takethenextstepcct.com. For groups, there is a one day retreat/workshop available. Contact me for details.

It would be my honor to help the real YOU stand up. It takes work, however, we will have fun in the process.

For your pondering

> *"This is my life. It is my one time to be me. I want to experience every good thing."—Maya Angelou*

> *"You were born an original. Don't die a copy." —John Mason*

> *"Why not have the real YOU stand up?" —Jane Bishop*

Jane Bishop

Jane Bishop is the founder and owner of Take The Next Step, which emerged out of her passion to help others "go for their It." She is known as someone who lives forward. Jane's passion for life and encouraging others is evident, whether chatting with a friend over a cup of coffee, brainstorming with a leadership team, or addressing hundreds of professionals from a platform. Her authenticity, enthusiasm, and innate desire to keep it all about the other person, provides the foundation for a captivating experience.

Recognized as an energetic speaker and trainer, Jane stirs her audiences with a "not to be forgotten" style, blending her teaching skills, experience and sense of humor. She challenges participants with powerful messages of opportunity and action. Her background of travel and change early in life as a military dependent has served her well and has allowed her to work with diverse populations across the United States.

Jane holds degrees from three institutions, has attained the Associate Certified Coach (ACC) credential, is a certified trainer for Basic Coaching Skills, and a DISC trainer/assessor. She is part of the virtual faculty of Coaching4Todays Leaders/Coaching4Clergy. Jane has written for numerous periodicals, is a contributing author in a seminary textbook and actively volunteers in her church and community. She is a life-long learner following her belief that "when a person stops learning, they stop living."

Jane Bishop
Life Coach, Speaker, Author
Take The Next Step
404-432-2701
jane@takethenextstepcct.com
www.takethenexstepcct.com

Moira Ní Ghallachóir

Aspire to Inspire — How to Live Your Dreams by Building a Freedom-Fueled Business (that takes worries about money off your plate)

On paper, I had all of the boxes checked.

The apartment in the world's most thrilling city. Exquisite dinners at restaurants. A closet full of clothes, the designer handbags and the shoes. Yet even with a life so full of invitations and important things, something lingered, leaving me feeling empty and lacking.

Up until four years ago, I had a full-time office job working at a nonprofit with young people in London preventing them from becoming homeless, and before that I worked in sales. It was an ultra fast-paced city life filled with jet setting, parties, and fashion shows. My parents back home in Ireland were proud of me, and against all measures, it seemed like I should be happy.

But instead, I felt uninspired and stuck.

I needed inspiration. I needed...*Paris.*

It was then that I made a decision that changed my life and my business forever. I'm sharing this with you because I believe—from the bottom of my heart—that this shift in thinking will also change your life and business.

Today, everything is different. I'm a business coach who works with entrepreneurs to build the thriving businesses they've always wanted, but that they didn't think they could have. I share my story in the hope that you find something within it that ignites something inside of you—and that you learn to use inspiration to create the life you've always wanted.

Do you ever find yourself wondering what it would be like to live the life of your dreams? Do you feel like there's something more waiting for you—a life of filled with passion, adventure and fulfillment, that is free from the worries of how you're going to pay for it?

This is the life I live now. I'm my own boss. My business has not only transformed my life, but my client's lives and even my hometown. I quadrupled my income in the past three years, and I am a sought-after speaker who travels internationally several times a year.

But as I began to explain, it wasn't always this way. My whole life changed only five short years ago, and I am so glad that it did.

The year I turned 36, my life felt like a display window of a closed store. It all looked nice on the outside, but it felt empty. The indecision of what to do next and where to go built up inside of me until I had to do something dramatic to escape.

Right after my birthday, I hopped on the Eurostar to Paris (the city of lights and romance) to sort out where to go next. I left everyone and everything I had built in London behind, and jumped into the freshness of a Paris, alive with possibility.

It's often in these moments of freedom and adventure that inspiration comes. Whether it's in life or in business, you must break away in order to break through. In my case, inspiration struck, in an unmistakably Irish accent.

I sat at a Parisian cafe, sipping cafe au lait and making lists—of jobs, of places to move to and of new possibilities. Nothing felt right, or like what I needed. Finally, I heard a small voice in the back of my mind whispering, "Donegal".

Until I was 18, I had lived in Donegal, in northwest Ireland. As soon as I could, I began traveling the world, building homes in Budapest, Madrid, and New York before settling in London where I had been living for the past six years.

I had honestly never entertained the thought of moving home. Growing up, I couldn't wait to leave. But here I was, croissant crumbs and my journal, and the thought of going back to Ireland flooded me with a feeling of peace. Clearly, my heart was on board.

My mind raced with a hundred questions; "What the hell? How can this happen? What about a job? Where will I live?" My brain wanted all the details sorted out beforehand. However, they would have to get sorted out later, because I was already decided. Ireland was calling me home, and I was answering.

There was less than a month in between cities. I came back to London from my Parisian adventure, and left my 9–5 job. I bought a small car and began to pack the most essential belongings of my life into it. Over the next two weeks, I said goodbye to the roaring London city-life, and drove the 11 hours to my Irish countryside hometown.

As I drove to Donegal, I was immediately filled with an overwhelming sense of peace, excitement and freedom. I'm so glad that I was, because I still didn't have any of the answers! The contrast of what would be my new pace of life settled in slowly as I drove. I recalled the sense of appreciation I felt taking in my country's natural landscapes. Once I arrived, things started falling into place. Even my grandmother's cottage that had been vacant for 40 years, suddenly became available for me to live in.

I was struck with an overwhelming sense of love for the natural beauty of Donegal. The area is nicknamed Ireland's "cradle of culture" for good reason. The air around me was filled with tones of Gaelige. The whole town was also wildly creative—everyone is either a singer, artist or musician. Add that to the scenery of beautiful mountains, lush green valleys, and glistening lakes and naturally, I felt wildly inspired.

Yet all around me, I saw under-appreciated potential, creativity, and beauty. The townspeople were struggling, businesses were closing, and many were moving away in search of something new. It was all because people didn't realize the level of beauty and potential in front of them.

The small-town authenticity was what made of Donegal so special. However, at the same time the town felt stuck in time. There were few tourists or visitors, so the energy felt stale. Having just come out of this feeling of stagnancy in my own life, I felt a resonance with the struggles of Donegal. I decided to leverage my excitement for the area to draw people to the area with a tourism-based business. I wanted to grow a business I loved while inspiring others to visit and have their own adventures.

My background in travel and sales provided me with the skills, and the landscape filled in the details. My mission was to rekindle the local people's passion for the place they lived, and to bring in international travelers for fresh new energy.

I took my message to the streets, getting a mixed response. Some locals were doubtful and resigned to the way things were. A lot of people asked me why I bothered trying. I heard reactions like, "Why don't you just find a job?" There was also the ever-popular query, "What happens if it doesn't work?" There were many excuses why people thought travelers wouldn't want to come here—such as the fact that we were in a deep recession, the weather, the location, etc.

Despite the doubt and skepticism, I had to stick to my intuition that told me to keep going. In truth, I knew something they didn't—that when you can be an inspiration to others, obstacles don't matter. I knew that I could tap into the power of inspiration to exponentially grow my sales, attract clients, and ultimately, grow a thriving business. That is exactly what happened. My attitude of excitement drew in more and more business. In only three short years, we brought over 1000 people to Donegal!

When other businesses saw how successful I was, they started to ask me for my help to grow theirs. I started coaching one, then another, and it just took off like that. I've gone from booking tours to leading retreats and coaching business owners worldwide on how to grow their businesses through inspiration-based sales, and in the process, quadrupling my income. My life now is filled with excitement. I get to speak at workshops and events in Ireland, England, and the US. I hold retreats here in my hometown designed to empower entrepreneurs. I'm now gearing up for my latest retreat—Ireland's first inspirational business retreat for women.

The amazing thing is—it all came from inspiration. It was not a script, formula, or something that felt awful or that I hated. It was something that was perfect for me. That's exactly what I see as possible for you.

The best part of this story is that my success was not unique to me. It is because when you use inspiration as your fuel, anything is possible. I have helped many entrepreneurs to achieve similar levels of success. I have made it my mission to empower entrepreneurs to create thriving businesses and lives they love, not through being pushy or salesy, but by naturally inspiring people.

Are you interested in learning how this can work for you?

When anyone asks me what the backbone of my approach is, I share a few things that I wish I had known from the start. These are my touchstones to creating a solid client base, driving profit, and creating more freedom for you and your business.

Here are the five powerful secrets. They are part of the curriculum I share at my women's business retreats that I would also love to share with you. These five steps will help you to create more income in a natural way, based on inspiring clients to see a greater vision of what is possible. If you can inspire people to see a bigger vision for themselves than they do, nothing will stand in your way.

Inspire Your Way to the Business of Your Dreams—My 5 Steps to Sales Success

Step 1: Believe in what you do.

When you are confident in what you offer, people will have more faith in what you deliver. As a result, you will get more clients. This is the most foolproof path to profits. The problem that I see most often is people think believing in themselves is self-centered. Despite what you might think, believing in what you're doing is NOT pushy, desperate, or salesy. It's actually *the most authentic way* to get more clients and to grow your business.

Step 2. Find out what your clients want.

Before you think about selling, you have to find out what your clients want. If you don't know, you're really gambling with your future. The problem is that most of us don't know what our clients really want. As a result, sales then become a nightmare of trying to "get them" to buy.

When you know what your clients want, selling is easy because you're giving them a faster path to what they're already looking for. This way, before you start, you're already 60% of the way to "Yes!" and your clients are receptive to offers.

Step 3. Position the outcome instead of the process.

Instead of talking about what you do, focus on what you make possible. Your client's interest will go through the roof. Let's test this out. Which sounds more enticing: "Work with me and I will walk you through a process and create a plan" OR "Work with me and double your profits and triple your time off." Do you see the difference?

I often hear that people are uncomfortable showing how they provide value. Show them how you will make an impact for them and they will start seeing you as a necessary step to get where they want to go. Your prospects aren't just investing in random stuff like a new television. They're investing in their dream.

Step 4. The Personal Touch: People buy from People

We are all human—we like to support people and brands that we trust. When you show up as who you are, you build trust with your audience. Being personal also makes you more memorable, and being memorable leads to more customers.

Some entrepreneurs believe that sounding "corporate", or bigger than you are is the key to profit. However, the truth is that this actually stands in your way. Most entrepreneurs are also afraid of picking up the phone and calling prospects, when it's actually the best way to connect with potential clients.

If you show your clients that you really care about their success, your sales will increase because your prospects are buying from someone they trust and connect with. People also know who you are and what you stand for, so they feel better about referring people to you.

Step 5. Consistency: Have a System that's designed for Success (and follow it!)

To make more money with less effort, you need a system that works for you. Too many business owners reinvent the wheel with every sale. That is tiring and leads to burnout. We're afraid that systems will make things more complicated, when in reality, they make things easier. *A business without a system is unsustainable.*

The important key is this: The fastest path to the business and life of your dreams does not depend on a complicated outside formula. It is based on what you're already good at, and what already makes your heart sing!

Want to inspire your way to a better life? Here's a gift! It's a downloadable guide that reveals the secrets I used to change my life. Use it and transform your business and life—in 30 days or less. You will find it at: www.mng.ie. You can also reach out to me via my site if you want to work together on building your business.

Getting clients by inspiring people, is the most personally gratifying and surefire formula to grow your business. My hope in sharing my story and these tools is that you incorporate the principle of "sales through inspiration" to build the business and live the deeply fulfilling life you've always dreamed of. Now, that is something to aspire to!

Moira Ní Ghallachóir

Moira helps small business owners and entrepreneurs who hate sales - inspire their way to more clients, customers and profits without being salesy. She wants them to have the increased profits they yearn for, that fuels a life they love ... doing what they love!"

She left her 9–5 job in London, to return home to Ireland to fulfill her dream of freedom by starting her own business. And in spite of having never owned a business before, she built a consistent 10K monthly revenue stream lightning fast, and now helps others to fulfill their dreams with their own profoundly profitable business.

Moira now brings her inspired, dynamic, successful brand of business mentoring to the U.S., to show American entrepreneurs a bigger vision for their own businesses, and a powerful, authentic path to inspire their way to more contacts, contracts, clients and cash! She also books one-of-a-kind business retreats to beautiful Donegal, for entrepreneurs to refresh, renew, and rediscover the power of their own business vision.

Moira Ní Ghallachóir
mng Ventures Ltd
51c Ranafast
Anagry, Co. Donegal Ireland
+353 83 123 0529 mngDonegal Skype
Moira@mng.ie
www.mng.ie

LoriAnne Reeves

It Turned Out to Be the Secret Sauce

I was listening intently to the conversation but the words were not computing in my brain. At first, I thought that it was a joke. Part of me started laughing inside. "You're kidding me, right?" What was going on? This conversation happened once before but that was over 25 years ago. We had come a long way. We were happy. Money hadn't been a problem for a long time. The last few years had been the best. Our kid was almost launched into independence. We were traveling. We were talking. We were laughing. This was crazy. I could not wrap my brain around, hear the words or comprehend what I was witnessing. This was not the person who I knew, trusted and loved. Most of all, it was not the person I respected. It was not perfect, but it was definitely a relationship built on love, respect and honesty. This was what I thought.

Yesterday was our anniversary. One day, you're happily married for 31 years. You are told how much you're loved and remember everything that encompassed your life together. The next day, he wanted a divorce. No one wants to hear someone else's sad story and I know I got very tired of hearing myself grieving, ruminating and being in complete shock. It felt like each week I was writing an episode of a novella on Telemundo. It was one epic discovery after another. In fact, even once the divorce was over, it took me a year to catch up with the story of my life from the previous year.

Prior to D-day, I had a successful marriage and family therapy practice for over twenty years. I had just shut it down to lead the expat life of travel and living and working abroad. Having commuted for the last two years, I was two weeks away from the big move. Today, I find the sad humor in realizing I was now caught up in the same situation that many of my clients found themselves experiencing. There was no grace period for adjustment to the fast paced events surrounding me and moving forward rapidly whether I was ready or not. While I was at my worst, I now needed to be my best in handling the fallout.

There was fallout I expected and fallout that I didn't. When you're married for over 30 years, there are expectations from others that this should not be happening after all this time. I couldn't disagree, but I had no answers for everyone. The taking sides didn't occur as much but the family was heartbroken. I was the designated caretaker for both sides of the family. Now in addition to them needing me, I needed them. It was quite the role reversal.

The biggest surprising fallout was from my married girlfriends who suddenly treated me as if I had contracted a contagious disease that they could catch. In the moment, it hurt me but now I get it. It could have easily happened to any of us because life just happens. They changed. Honestly, I was changed by this situation so they had no choice but to change towards me. In fact, it's an opportunity to reassess everything.

I was losing my marriage, way of life, friends, business, income, and knowing what I knew. However, I had a choice. Having your life break apart gives you the choice to see it as the beginning of a new chapter. Honestly, I can write that now. However, in the middle of my grief, the thought I had was that I didn't want to be bitter in the end. My private practice was full of folks like that who had life happen and they could never move forward even slightly.

Something like this doesn't happen in a vacuum. I spent many days thinking back and reassessing my life while taking care of all that needed to be done when a long term marriage dissolves. There were the highly practical items like finding a way to make money to pouring over paperwork that attorneys needed. When I say it didn't happen in a vacuum, I had plenty of alone time to ponder every nuance of myself and my background. It was a self-imposed alone time during which I wasn't always kind to myself. I've always taken care of everyone and now I was wondering how to take care of myself. It was time to go beyond the personal and all my emotions and look toward the conscious way I wanted to create myself and my life.

The truth was that I had hung onto my relationship, marriage, family and son with everything I had. I was not raised in a loving home. I don't mean that no one said, "I love you." It was a war zone to live in the house where my siblings and I grew up. It gives you a choice as to how you want to live your life in the future. As an adult, you can choose to pay attention and live purposely on purpose in the home and family life you create for yourself and those around you. It was a choice each day to have what you didn't have as a child. I often shared with the clients in my private practice that as an adult, you have the opportunity to heal from the past by creating for your children the life you didn't have. In that space, you get to break generational binds so they no longer are passed on to the next generation.

My adult life began when I went to college on a scholarship that was in a degree that I would not have chosen for myself. However, it was close enough. I had a deep desire for an education and I found a way to pay for it. In my mind, education was freedom and the opportunity to earn the kind of money to live where I wanted. It didn't help that there was a recession going on when I graduated. Jobs were scare for everyone. I interviewed and was offered a good job in the Midwest. This Rhode Island gal felt like she was in a foreign country when no one understood her when asking, "Where's the bubbler?" FYI—that's a water fountain.

Married now and with a move to Texas, life was good with great jobs and a house in a neighborhood that embraced us. They didn't mind our non-native status among them. It was home and we had tons of family visiting over the years to attend the rodeo and eat Tex-Mex. We converted a few of them to even try to living here. Family started to wonder when those babies were coming and so did both of us. After 8 years of infertility treatment and many miscarriages, our son was born through IVF. He may have been difficult to conceive but I am so grateful to have witnessed the adult man he has become. Life was good and it got better as the years unfolded. Those last years with just the two of us, felt almost like when we first met.

You might be thinking what I was thinking. If it was so great, how did you end up with a divorce after all those years together? I searched for the answer for a long time and have decided that I'll never get the answer to why. What I knew in the moment was that my traditional life no longer existed and I would need to again choose how I wanted to live my life. The problem was that I was a mess.

There are so many folks out there who are in worse situations than you are. However, your grief is yours, so take the time you need to move through your feelings while you take even the smallest step forward. You get to feel your feelings not live your feelings. With that in mind, I needed to assess my situation. I had been an entrepreneur since the 1980's. No corporation was going to hire me for the money I wanted and I was worried about my age being a factor. There was lots of advice from family and friends. I could just get any old job and wait out the years until social security. That actually made me angry. Were they unconsciously telling me I was no longer viable? That was unacceptable for me. If I was reinventing myself, I wanted to be all of me.

I needed to pull in the one skill I knew was the secret sauce that I have relied on my entire life. Sometimes it's called grit, sometimes it's called having the guts and sometimes folks think you're just crazy. Whatever you call it, having *resilience* in your life and business is what gets you to where you want to go to create the lifestyle for you and your family. I would take all of my skills and step into this coaching world that I had never heard of until now. I would create a business that would support me in how I wanted to be supported. It's still a work in progress. I'm here to tell you that I made mistakes, invested in myself, and didn't always trust my instincts. I took calculated risks that would grip me with fear and I took them anyway.

Fear never goes away. You just get friendly with fear and you realize that it's an indication that you are resisting change or you are about to take your next leap. I see this many times with my own clients when they refuse to step into that next thing they need to grow personally and professionally. I tell them they are letting fear or ego get in the way. This is what I know about resistance and fear. It is that you will not be able to find your resilience to hang in there for your next step in your journey, if it controls you. It's resilience that is the special gift which gets you to your next goal, that next step, the new client and the money flowing into your life. The combination of passion, action and resilience is the secret sauce behind success, especially for entrepreneurs. You can have all the passion, desire and creativity. However, if you are not resilient in your journey, it can be a game changer in how long you last and how successful you'll be, especially in your own business. This is because everything is magnified.

It doesn't mean you go it alone as in "pull up your bootstraps." Being resilient is knowing when to get support. I needed support on this new journey of mine. I hired a coach. I paid out my contract because it wasn't a good fit. I hired another coach. I was still messy. This is because starting over and reinventing yourself is not linear. It's not about giving up. When you do this inner work, you change. Change has consequences. Not everyone will still be there with you but others come into your life that are there for your new journey. Those that stay with you are your greatest supporters.

I'm still reinventing and figuring it out. However, along the way, I've created a business that I love. Helping my clients stop playing small and stepping into who they are as passionate human beings and creating the lifestyle for them is exciting. I've met new friends and colleagues and I've traveled. I had forgotten how much I enjoyed traveling and having fun experiences. My relationship with my son is in a new, wonderful and grown up place. He is my biggest supporter. Some days I work harder than others but it has an ease and flow and rhythm to it. There were no directions in how to ride this crazy wave

I was on for the last few years. However, each exploration of how this could support my next step, no matter how small, could be in service of myself and others.

LoriAnne Reeves

LoriAnne Reeves is a serial entrepreneur who has had a varied career over the last 24 years. It has come together in a way that now serves her clients at the highest level. From her first entrepreneurial service as the best babysitter to her current businesses, LoriAnne teaches, coaches, mentors and speaks in both the entrepreneurial and creative space.

LoriAnne started her entrepreneurial journey early, at the age of 11, as an in demand babysitter and selling Barbie clothes that she created. Many adventures, jobs and business attempts led to a full scholarship to college. Upon graduation, LoriAnne entered the corporate world where she received Salesperson of the Year Award. After a complete switch to graduate school, she started a Marriage & Family Therapy practice. Besides seeing her own clients, LoriAnne supervised other therapists for certification, coached them in creating six figure incomes, and consulted with Fortune 100 companies on crisis management, international relocations and team dynamics.

As a Business Strategist and Coach, LoriAnne serves her clients through not only the outer game of business strategy but also the inner game of getting out of their own way so that the transformation and business success can happen. One of her areas of expertise, is helping clients to rewrite their money story in life and business so that clients can have the financial success and lifestyle they want and desire.

Mistakes, detours and unexpected life events has shaped and led LoriAnne to give her clients leadership with the one ingredient necessary in life and business—resilience.

LoriAnne lives in Friendswood, Texas and has a 26 year old son who is financially independent. (Yeah!)

LoriAnne Reeves

The CEO Entrepreneur

203 Falcon Lake Dr.

Friendswood, TX 77546

281-381-9270

LoriAnne@LoriAnneReeves.com

www.LoriAnneReeves.com

Jen Coffel & Kim Bavilacqua
HOPE: Trials and Triumphs

One guarantee in life is that it is full of peaks and valleys. There are seasons of trials and triumphs. That's why the book of James 1:2–4 says "Consider it pure joy, my brothers and sisters, whenever you face trials of many kinds, because you know the testing of your faith produces perseverance. Let perseverance finish its work so that you may be mature and complete, not lacking anything."

What does that kind of life look like? To be mature in Christ not lacking for anything? We imagine it is a life filled with HOPE. Over the last decade, we have learned a great deal about trials, triumphs and great HOPE. We have also learned we may be able to live without food or water for a certain amount of time but we absolutely cannot live without hope. Our desire after you read this is that you will be filled with hope to be able to trust deeply, believe for the things you think are impossible, and persevere through the storm until the skies are sunny once again.

We are no strangers to the storms in life. We met at a moms' group at church. We were in the season of parenting young children. Jen had four children under the age of three and Kim had a three year old daughter. Looking back, we see it was not by mistake that we were seated at the same table and formed a fast friendship. Although we had no idea all what God had in store, one thing was certain. He would use our lives as a testimony of hope.

KIM'S STORY

When I met Jen I was in the process of a divorce. My world was turned upside down. I needed to move. I needed to find a job. I had no idea how I was going to be able to do that with a three year old. It was a place of crying out to God for answers and trusting him when I could not see the forest for the trees. The desire of my heart was to be at home to raise my daughter. Her birth was truly a miracle. We both almost died and I knew she would be my only child. When I met Jen, I needed hope. As a single mom, I felt that I had no real plan for starting over. Jen shared with me a way that I could work from home. We began working together. That was the first time I saw God knitting us together for a bigger purpose. He was faithful to give me the desire of my heart; to be there every day for my daughter. I'm going to let Jen tell you the rest of the story.

JEN'S STORY

When I met Kim, I was new to the area and did not know very many people. The reality of my life was this: I had a 3 year old, 2 year old twins and a newborn and I was exhausted. I had struggled for 6 years with unexplained infertility. After adopting our first daughter, I chose to sell my driver rehab practice because I really wanted to be at home to raise her. Then I had twins by in vitro. I contracted a bad infection after giving birth and had to be hospitalized. A year passed and I was still struggling with health complications, so I began seeking out holistic healthcare for answers. During this time we were about $1000 short each month in paying our bills. I wasn't prepared for all the costs associated with adoption, in vitro and raising children in general. I started looking for a way to work from home. I discovered a wellness company that not only provided me with information about creating a healthy home, but it gave me hope.

It was hope that I could be at home with my children and help other moms do the same. God blessed me with the ability to do just that. When I met Kim, I was so excited to share it with her because I knew we both wanted the same things; to work from home, be with our children, live well and teach other moms that they could too.

Kim and I had been working together for two years teaching wellness and helping moms create healthy homes. Then life threw us a curveball and Kim was diagnosed with cancer. So you can imagine the shock we both felt. For Kim, as a single mom having to battle cancer, fear was her biggest enemy. Her biggest fear was that the cancer would claim her life and she would not be able to see her three year old daughter grow up. She desperately wanted to complete the purpose God had given her. We made the decision to completely trust God and began praying daily for healing and peace. I witnessed fear and anxiety be replaced by trust and peace in Kim's life. A cancer battle is a huge trial and clinging to the promise of hope is the triumph.

As Kim began feeling better, we started really contemplating the call on our lives. How could we make a big impact for Christ? What was His purpose and plan? He led us over and over to the word HOPE. We also kept coming back to the cancer community. Kim knew from a survivor standpoint why she was passionate about cancer prevention. I attributed my passion to knowing the cancer statistics and not wanting my children to be at risk. We co- authored an educational awareness program called the No Toxin Zone. The program teaches people the truth about toxins and how they can reduce their risk of disease.

We also designed a corporate wellness program and started a non -profit called Handing H.O.P.E. H.O.P.E. is an acronym for Helping others through Prevention and Education. It also stands for Helping Others through Provision and Evangelism. We began working on our first project and then life threw us three more curveballs. And they were huge ones. First, my best friend Jennifer was diagnosed with brain cancer. I was her power of medical attorney and attended all of her appointments for three years. Within the time of her treatment, my dad was diagnosed with lung cancer and my mom with pancreatic cancer. I lost my dad first, then my mom and then Jennifer. I was completely devastated. The three most important people in my life, those who loved me the deepest, were gone. The pain was indescribable. To say I felt shattered, doesn't even scratch the surface. It was hard to want to wake up and face the day without them in it. My parents were my biggest cheerleaders. I experienced unconditional love from them. That kind of love, when you stop receiving it, leaves an enormous void in your life. I shut down. I worked minimally. The ministry of Handing H.O.P.E. was put on hold.

For two years, I allowed God to put me back together day by day. I trusted Him at first to just help me get out of bed. Then He helped me to heal my physical body from the toll grief takes. He then restored my hope. He knew all those years ago when He gave me a passion for the cancer community that I was going to lose my parents and Jennifer to cancer. In my storm, He continually met my needs and healed my wounds. In the very same way, He did for Kim in her battle with cancer. Our hope came from knowing He never lets our trials be for nothing. Romans 8:28 says "and we know all matters work together for good for those who love God and are called according to *His* purpose." We trust Him in His infinite wisdom and plan for us with confidence in knowing He always has our best interest at heart. This is where we have seen our trials become our triumphs. It gives us great hope to know that His word says He will never leave or forsake us.

And He hasn't. We weathered the storms and God has returned us to our work with Handing H.O.P.E. He knit our passions, trials and burdens into our purpose. In a short time, we have seen many triumphs. First, we began our Lollipop tree project with a vision of bringing healthy naturally sugar free lollipops to children's cancer clinics nationwide. At the time of this writing, we have trees located in five states and more requests happening daily. Illinois alone has nine trees planted. Our second triumph was to become authors. We have written a book *Be Well Assured: At the Heart of Cancer there is HOPE*. The book brings inspiration and education. We seek to honor God, and consider our biggest triumph to be stay at home working moms serving our families each day.

Looking back, things could have been very different. If we had never found hope in our trials, we would never know the victory of triumph. Hope is truly the anchor to the soul. When we couple hope with faith; faith being the confidence in what we hope for and the assurance in what we do not see; God can turn trials into triumphs.

What are the trials you are facing today? Do you have a dream or vision that you feel is impossible? Matthew 7:7 says, "Ask and it shall be given to you; seek, and you shall find; knock, and it shall be opened to you." Believe God always has your best interest at heart. Have faith to know he has a plan for you and that nothing is too big for Him. He is a God of miracles. You are the child of a King. You can approach His throne room with bold prayers. He will pour out his wisdom. You just have to listen and follow His instruction. Then praise Him in advance, for you will see your trial transformed into triumph.

Connect with Jen and Kim:

Visit www.HandingHope.org and like us on Facebook

Visit www.NoToxinZone.com for more about prevention

Jen Coffel

Jen Coffel is the co-founder of Handing H.O.P.E. She is responsible for the vision, strategy and national fundraising efforts for Handing H.O.P.E and the Lollipop tree project as it expands across the country.

"If you believe it, you can achieve it" is Jen's mantra in life.

Jen lost her dad, mom and best friend to cancer in a less than two year period. Out of her loss and grief, she found her passion to make a difference in the lives of those battling cancer.

Jen is an author and speaker. She has been featured and recognized on ABC News and the Chicago Tribune for her work in helping others. Her innovative and down to earth style sets her audience at ease and empowers them to receive her message of wellness.

Jen has over a decade of experience in the wellness industry and a Bachelor's Degree from University of Illinois at Chicago. She is also the co-author of *Be Well Assured—At the Heart of Cancer There is H.O.P.E.*

Jen Coffel

Handing Hope NFP

15280 Jughandle Rd.

Minooka, IL 60447

815-690-9095

admin@handinghope.org

www.HandingHope.org

Kim Bavilacqua

Kim Bavilacqua is the co-founder of Handing H.O.P.E. As a cancer survivor, she knows the battle that these children face. The lollipop tree allows her to bring hope and smiles to these children!

With a Bachelors of Social Work, Kim has been teaching wellness for 10 years. As a co-author of the awareness program, The No Toxin Zone, Kim is able to share her passion for helping others to be proactive about their own health through prevention and education.

A "master planner," Kim's expertise is in organizing and implementing corporate events and wellness workshops. Her humor and zest for life shines through as she shares the message of HOPE!

Kim is also the co-author *Be Well Assured—At the Heart of Cancer There is H.O.P.E.*

Kim Bavilacqua
Handing Hope NFP
info@handinghope.org
www.HandingHope.org

Nichole Santoro

Face Your Fears and Embrace What's Next

I delivered my mom's eulogy after she had passed away due to cancer at the age of 51. 11 years later, I spoke at a local community memorial service, sharing memories of my dad after he passed of a massive stroke at age 66. Neither of my parents had the chance to "grow old." I have no regrets, no "things left unsaid," just the sadness of losing my biggest fans and cheerleaders. How was I supposed to move on and to continue living life in spite of such profound grief and sadness?

My sister, dad and I all spent time and stayed with my mom for the two weeks before she passed, never leaving her side. If there are angels on Earth, hospice workers are among them. Our lovely hospice nurse talked us through everything that was happening, what to expect, and helped navigate our fears and questions. Even now as I reflect on the intensity of my feelings and pain, I have since come to realize there are always people here to support and guide you, once you let them in. The days after my mom died, I'd wake and think, "OK, I'm here, I'm still alive. Now what do I do?" I'd say to myself, "I'm going to get out of bed and put one foot in front of the other and I'm going to work." And I did.

The day I got back to work, I was showered with cards, love and good wishes. My generous co-workers took time out of their busy schedules to give me the strength to keep going. My dad, sister and I would get together each weekend to write thank you cards, go through pictures, and to figure out "what was next" for each of us. As the days turned into weeks and we started moving on, the three of us would schedule weekly "conference calls" where we'd reminisce and just talk to each other. I'm so grateful for the time that we had together to bond. As time went on, my dad took on the role of "our mom" while my sister and I would share all these stories with him about everything happening in our life. My dad finally asked during one of our marathon conference calls, "Did your mother listen to all of this? Is it OK if I don't remember everyone's names?" Boy, did we start cracking up. We said "yes"…and then we KEPT ON TALKING. How funny this all seems in retrospect! I'm incredibly grateful for that additional time with my dad to help deal with the grief of losing my mom. Years later, I would unexpectedly be saying goodbye to the man who called me, "Nikki-Nik."

While my sister and I were dealing with our grief, my dad had been dealing with his own. Since they were married in their early 20's, my parents grew up together. My dad was trying to navigate how he'd spend his remaining time without my mom. He ultimately moved west to a very small town called Mt. Carroll, IL. He spent the next 10+ years, giving 110% of himself by volunteering in the community, and opening and running a local coffee shop. He hosted open mic nights and served copious amounts of food and coffee. He frequently organized and ran Mt. Carroll events to entertain the local community and to generate visibility for all the local businesses. He gave, gave and gave some more to the adopted community that he adored. When my family would visit him, we'd joke that he was the local celebrity since it appeared that virtually everyone in the city knew him. My dad was burning the candle at both ends. But none of us could fault him—Mt. Carroll was HIS healing and his place where he now belonged. This was the group of people he welcomed into his life to support him, just as much as he poured his heart and soul into their town. The community quickly learned all about my mom (whom they never met), as well as his daughters, sons-in-law, and grandson (whom they did meet!). My dad was a gregarious man who was an equally gifted listener and very interesting and entertaining conversationalist – he felt right at home at his coffee shop!

There's a fortitude and perseverance that comes from overcoming grief, struggle and pain. I've definitely lost tolerance for what I see as senseless drama. (Just kiss and make up already—time is shorter than we think!) But we don't get stronger by ourselves. My dad grew stronger once he opened his heart to an incredible new community. I grew stronger sharing story after story with my husband, who has comforted me many times in the days and years that followed. I grew stronger once I had my son. I was completely blown away at the miracle of life and the feelings of astounding joy watching him grow. It is an experience that words simply can't capture. I've been surrounded by my loving family and friends for whom I'm incredibly grateful. I have also become aware of an industry of people who serve in the world to lift us up, show what's possible, help navigate our fears, and remove the barriers (largely self-imposed!) to create a vision and make positive things happen in our own lives.

About a year after my mom died, I was going to work every day but wasn't sure what I should do next. I just had a feeling of general un-rest and didn't know why. I began a binge of reading self-help books, beginning with *What Color Is Your Parachute.* I have now read so many that I couldn't even begin to list them all here. This was in 2005 when there was internet and email, but before social media. In my self-discovery journey, I learned about "career coaching." It involves actually hiring somebody and working with them over the phone to build the life that you dreamed of. I am still continually inspired by the experience of being coached. I haven't always had a coach over the years. However, I find that I can get past my own blocks and fears and actually make progress much faster towards my personal goals, whenever I have a coach in my corner. This inspired me to earn my own life and career coaching certifications. While I was pregnant, I offered life coaching to help career-oriented moms balance their life with kids, while meeting the demands of their careers. I eventually decided to continue with my marketing career. Nevertheless, my heart is with the coaching industry. I am continually amazed by the entrepreneurs who believe so passionately in what they do, that they've dedicated their lives to lifting and inspiring others.

I've often hired a coach for one reason (my business), but then it leads to other areas in my life that are holding me back. I find that I need to address these issues in order to move forward.

An example is my fear of flying. My sister and I were blessed that my grandparents took us to Disney World. Our flights were simply breathtaking. I took pictures of the clouds with their Kodak camera. I didn't fly again until my 20s. I was a little jittery but nothing more. When I lived in Glendale, California for a couple years, I flew cross-country a few times and never experienced anything out of the ordinary. Later in my career, I traveled for a photo shoot for my client. It was rather stormy, but somehow even after some delays, I returned home safely. That night was September 10, 2001. The next morning, I had to reassure concerned loved ones and colleagues that I had arrived home safely. Even then, my husband and I were inspired to travel and see New York the following month.

If 9/11 didn't do it, then what caused me to vow to not fly for a year? I even thought that I might never fly again. It was nothing more than a couple of wacky, turbulent flights going back and forth on vacation. On one particular flight, I felt like I was on the Millennium Falcon. (My husband was equally agitated, and my young son said simply, "Hmm, this ride is kind of bumpy.")

It took some time but reluctantly I did start flying again. Earlier this year, as part of the mastermind group that I joined, I had the opportunity to go to a retreat in the mountains in Canmore, a beautiful town in Alberta, Canada. I almost did not go due to flying jitters!

How did coaching help? I was working with 2 different coaches for support in a couple different areas of my business. I finally shared my shame with this "illogical fear" and asked for their support to deal with it.

They each helped me valiantly shine the light on my fear. They said that by making this choice, I'd also be inadvertently making other choices. By choosing NOT to fly, I'd be missing an incredible opportunity to see a part of the world I'd never seen. I would be choosing to put a ceiling on my business growth if I decided NOT to invest in my own leadership development. The most appalling thing was the fearful lesson I would be teaching my son. I would be telling him that it's NOT OK to live life full-out when you're scared. After considering all of this, I ultimately decided that it was NOT the message I want to live or to exemplify.

In the end, I flew to Canada, even on a smaller plane than my "typical minimum requirement." It was a MARVELOUS experience that allowed me to meet other incredibly talented business owners, I learned about tapping into courage when you don't yet have confidence. I was enamored with Earth's natural beauty that I hadn't seen at this level. While I was flying, I was in a constant state of gratitude that I even HAD this opportunity to enrich my life in such a profound way.

Life, health, business and career coaches have continually helped me to remove perceived obstacles and to get me back on track to live the life of my dreams. I have lost weight. I have let go of my wonderful full-time job in order to pursue the entrepreneurial journey. This has happened more than once! A year ago, if someone had said I'd attend a leadership mastermind retreat in the beautiful Canadian Rockies, I would've said, "Do I need to remind you that I'm afraid of flying?" If you'd said I'd be representing my own business at a trade show, I would've told you how I'm an introvert and that's not really my scene. I did the trade show just two weeks after my trip. It's exciting to watch what you can do when you hire a coach, face your fears, and really just go for it!

We all have dreams. As we evolve, our dreams also evolve. It's not a matter of overcoming one obstacle or meeting one achievement. Life is about learning, growing, desiring something, overcoming and achieving – again and again.

My next business goal is to build my podcast (internet radio show) to generate visibility and publicity for coaches and service-based businesses who want to make a difference in the world by helping people navigate their journeys and honor their dreams. It is also to share the stories of people in the business of bringing immense joy (or simply relief!) with their product or service. As a family, we want to "give back" as much as we can. My husband and I are now exploring fostering a child, and hope that it will be a way that we can shine some more fun and lightheartedness in the world.

There's so much that's good in the world. The possibilities are endless. I can't wait to see what comes next!

Nichole Santoro

Nichole Santoro is a Podcast Specialist and Owner of iMarketingSalon, LLC. Her 20+ year marketing career includes working with Nestlé, the United States Postal Service and Clear Channel Radio. As a trusted confidante, Nichole helps success-oriented business professionals to build relationships with new prospects, influencers, and referral partners by developing and executing a consistent marketing plan with podcasting, blogging, social media and email list building. From 2012–2013, Nichole hosted 24 podcast episodes of "Get Social, Coach!", where guests asked questions and learned about social media marketing strategies. Nichole currently hosts the podcast, "Biz and Tell" on BlogTalkRadio.com to shine the spotlight on coaches, speakers and service-based entrepreneurs on the fast-track to success. These are individuals who are committed to providing an excellent service for their clients and dedicated to making incredible strides in the world! For fun and rejuvenation, Nichole loves spending time with her husband and son at baseball games, local carnivals, wacky and fun 5K races, Disney vacations, road trips and even Midwest staycations.

Nichole Santoro

iMarketingSalon, LLC

P.O. Box 418

Elmhurst, IL 60126-0418

630-379-1395

Nichole@iMarketingSalon.com

www.iMarketingSalon.com

Margie Goliak

The Roadmap of Life

There are certain things in life that I have always gravitated towards. Some of these include school because I like the routine of it, and a love of cooking and sewing which allows me to express my creative side. When I reflect on why I have always enjoyed these things, I realize that they all have the same key characteristic. If you follow the instructions, rules, and process, you'll get a decent result. It seemed obvious to me at a young age that life had a roadmap or set of instructions.

I have learned from Tony Robbins about having a blueprint or roadmap for your life. Many of us set up the roadmap. When things go differently than planned, it can lead to unhappiness. My roadmap looked something like this … find the love of your life in college, get a cozy apartment near Wrigley Field, home of the Chicago Cubs, take the famous Chicago "L" downtown to a tall high rise, and live happily ever after. I was lucky enough for the first part of my roadmap to match my reality. The work part, however, was not what I expected. The confines of a corporate job were not interesting to me. I could not be in an office all day because I love to meet new people, and I like my independence. Sales seemed like a good fit, but I found myself in the extremely male dominated construction industry selling electrical equipment. It was clearly the old boys club, and I did not fit in at all. Even though it was 2002, suppliers were still taking the sales force out to strip bars at lunch. It was clear that I was not invited to many of these events (which was fine with me —I had better taste in lunch options). In 2003 I gave birth to my first son, and it seemed like a great time to take a break from the workforce. Suddenly, my roadmap didn't fit at all. I embraced being a stay at home mom, but I thought it would be a temporary situation, and that I would easily transition back to a corporate sales job. I had two more gorgeous sons. My husband traveled, and I dedicated myself to a happy home for my little tribe.

I continued to follow the roadmap and instructions for what I thought would be this phase of my life. Motherhood, however is a great reminder that things don't always go as planned. Until I became a mom, I, of course, had no idea how much work three children could be. I continued to give and give more to my family. I enjoyed creating joy for my family, but what I thought would be a temporary break from corporate life turned into 10 years in the blink of an eye. The constant demand of taking caring of my kids was not enough to keep me excited about life and help me move forward. I knew that at some level, returning to work was going to happen. I longed for a sustainable position that would cater to the flexibility and independence I desired, but I still wanted a job that would challenge me and keep me learning.

I'll never forget one particular fall day in 2012. Late September is a wonderful time where we live. The leaves are turning, and we are often blessed with one last blast of warm summer air. Fall always bring with it the idea of change and new beginnings. I loved the beginning of a new school year. To me the changing leaves were just a parallel to making changes in life. My oldest and middle sons were now in school, and my youngest was going to be starting preschool. I could almost feel that a new chapter of my life was about to start. This next chapter would not be dedicated to preschool, naptime, and chicken nuggets. I was scouring through brochures for local community colleges to see if there was a great career option for me. Once again, I was lacking an exact roadmap of what to do next.

A friend had asked me to check out her network marketing business, and I quickly dismissed the request. I had a belief that there was no way to be successful in the direct selling industry. I would soon see how wrong I was. Her product did not intrigue me, but I have to admit the idea of working from home, getting back to my sales routes, and learning new things sparked a new awakening in my soul. My husband and I were casually discussing the direct selling industry, when we both wondered if there was a direct seller of quality wine. We traveled to wine country, visited wineries on vacation, and certainly loved a good bottle of red. Nowhere in my life roadmap did I predict I would be in the home party business. In fact, I wouldn't even go to a home party to shop. However, the winds of change were blowing, and thanks to Google I did some quick research. After some online looking, a personal conversation with a great company, and a desire to try something new, I decided to be a wine consultant and offer in home wine tastings.

My original plan was to keep it simple. Time was precious for me, just like everyone else. I had three young children, my husband was an amazing provider and traveled quite a bit, and we never seemed to have a free night! I honestly believed this would be a great way to exercise some the of the business skills that I had been neglecting. An at home business was a great way to practice work force skills. After all, I hadn't been in an office since 2002, and as we all know, technology changes quickly. When I got an email with a document attached I felt nervous because I didn't know how to download that document. When I hopped on board as a wine consultant, it required a very small *financial* commitment, but it did require a lot of personal commitment to learn new things. Little did I know that this adventure would lead to so many lessons learned, great rewards, and constant growth.

I spent the first couple of months in my business sticking to the basics. I discovered very quickly that the roadmap for success in my industry had already been discovered. I just had to replicate the exact same thing other successful people were doing. Were some of the necessary steps going to challenge me to get outside of my comfort zone? Absolutely! I had knowledge of sales, but direct selling is a huge industry with best practices. I'm a busy mom, and I didn't have time to reinvent the wheel. I just followed the program and instructions of great leaders.

My plan to keep it simple was being challenged. My husband's work schedule continued to keep him traveling on weekdays, my children were experiencing some challenges that required lots of visits to specialists, and I was booking three or more tastings each week. I had no roadmap to figure this all out. I did realize, however, that if I just kept learning and growing, I could make my own roadmap. There was power in being able to design my own roadmap for life.

The first few months into my business, I experienced the power of "Setting your intentions" as a way to start to build my own roadmap. In my 4 years at college and my 10 years in corporate America, I had never even heard about the importance of goal setting. I always associated goals with New Year's Eve and weight loss. After less than three months into the start of my business, I was very close to my first promotion. To earn this promotion, I needed to sell $900 more in product, and that seemed like a massive goal to me. It was December 23. I had only 7 days to make the sales. I had no wine tastings coming up, I had no time to make phone calls, and I was leaving in a few days for a family vacation. My director at the time encouraged me by telling me, "Margie, just write $900 on a sticky note, and put it on your bathroom mirror". I groaned and promised to take this one easy step. It was very close to Christmas, and my neighbor was hosting a Christmas party. I showed up with a great bottle of wine. I was lucky enough to run into a guest, and we talked about my business. I shared a great glass of wine with him to celebrate the holiday season. He loved what I was offering, and he committed to buying at least 12 bottles of wine from me the next day. My head said not to call this stranger and follow through since it was Christmas Eve, but my ambition took over. I dropped by his house on Christmas Eve with my kids waiting in the minivan. I walked out of the house $350 closer to my goal. The goal seemed very attainable! I found the courage to dial up clients and make the rest of the sales to earn the promotion. This was start of stretching to reach goals. I call this story the power of the sticky note, and how incredible it is when you open yourself up to opportunity everywhere.

I know one thing for sure - serving my clients and treating them to an individualized wine tasting gave me much joy. I approached each event with enthusiasm and customization. I thrived on watching my guests spend quality time with friends and family that they don't get to see often. I'll never forget one night when I was in the kitchen of a new hostess. She lived about an hour away from me, and I had met her at a previous event. We were sipping on sparkling when two of my favorite clients from my community walked in the door. They drove over an hour to come to this tasting. When we sat down they declared to the room, "We didn't just come for the wine, we came to be with Margie!" I continue this same enthusiasm to this date. It doesn't matter to me if I pull up to a million dollar home or a small one bedroom condo. Every clients gets the best service I can deliver.

The hidden gem in my direct selling experience has been the joy of watching others succeed. Working with other consultants across the country and in my area is what keeps me motivated. I never dreamed that I would make friends and be able to visit with them on vacations! I'll never forget the joy of working with a team member who was achieving more than she thought possible. Her medical debt was erased thanks to the money she was earning, and this was a burden she never thought she would get rid of. She was now able to be debt free AND she was loving the work along the way. More than anything, the joy of helping others is what keeps me going day to day.

When I was a working in the corporate world, I only dreamed of another option. However, when you drive through traffic every day and sit in a cubicle, you are numb to the idea that there are other options. Through this industry, I have met the most amazing people. I have met people who have broken out of the norm by redefining their lives and becoming things like realtors, insurance agents, writers, and caterers (to name just a few). Everyone has a story. The more people I meet, the more I realize that everyone has something that could be holding them back—chronic illnesses, parents that need care, children with special needs, or devastating accidents. Even things that are not obvious are trying to hold all of us back—fear of the unknown, lack of belief in ourselves, and insecurities. Most people do not get to lead a life with a perfect roadmap. When we accept a change in our roadmap with joy and a desire to adapt, we can truly create freedom and happiness. I'm constantly amazed and inspired by those who don't let uncontrollable life issues get in their way. It is way too easy to get caught up in day to day life. Working in this business has shown to me that there is another way. It is amazing to wake up and realize with a clear goal, pure joy, and commitment for helping others, I can set the direction and roadmap for my own life. I see way too many people waiting for life to happen. I believe now that we can make the life we want happen.

Margie Goliak

Margie Goliak is an Independent Wine Consultant for WineShop at Home, a licensed, bonded winery in Napa, California. She began her journey in 2012, and quickly fell in love with both the company's exclusive artisan wines and the wine lifestyle! In her first year of business, Margie was honored with the prestigious Rising Star Award. This award is presented to a new Wine Consultant who has shown the most growth in their first year of business. From that moment on, she continued to earn many of the company's awards and achievements—from top in sales and recruiting to leader development. In 2015, Margie was awarded the company's prestigious President's Achievement Award, honoring the Wine Consultant who best exemplifies the company president's high standards for excellence and personal ethics. Margie proudly and enthusiastically leads a nationwide team of independent Wine Consultants, and her greatest joy is found in helping others to achieve their own personal success.

When Margie is not busy working with her team or treating her clients to a private wine tasting, she can be found taking care of her three boys and her husband of 20 years. The entire Goliak family shares a passion for travel and they feel blessed to travel frequently together to favorite destinations such as Michigan and the beautiful mountains of Colorado. Margie has also traveled the world to exotic destinations, earning her company's luxury incentive trips many times throughout her successful career. Margie credits her success to her love of learning and networking. Whether she's reading or listening to a podcast, Margie loves to absorb the best of the best to broaden her knowledge. Of course, one of her greatest loves of all is what she calls living the wine country lifestyle—creating special memories by sharing food, conversation and great wine with family and friends.

Margaret Goliak
WineShop at Home
630-217-9416
margiewine@yahoo.com
www.margiegoliak.com

Lisa Rexroad

A Hope of a New Tomorrow

One of my favorite life quotes is "Life is a journey, not a destination" by Ralph Waldo Emerson. It really does sum up my life. We all have a story to tell—good or bad, long or short, funny or sad. Here is mine from the heart. Thanks in advance for reading it!

I'm the older of two daughters from a "middle class" family who lived in the northwestern suburbs of Chicago. My Dad worked at one of the largest railroads in downtown Chicago for 29 years. He was the youngest of four brothers and had a very difficult childhood. He worked hard, but suffered from depression. He would come into my room during school nights and talk about suicide, how horrible his life was and that I shouldn't get married. I felt bad for him and looked forward to the days when he would smile and laugh. My Mom stayed at home to raise my sister and me. She was a phone solicitor and asked for donations (clothing) for the American Veterans. She relied quite heavily on my Dad. He was very controlling and that generation was known for being old fashioned…"the man works and the woman stays home". She didn't drive and had to ask him for permission on certain things. My Dad carried his childhood baggage that controlled and ultimately destroyed him. He and my Mom would argue relentlessly. I remember telling my Mom during one of their bad arguments to get a divorce. However, she wouldn't since it would be hard on us girls and because she wasn't financially independent. As I grew up, I saw these behaviors in my parents and vowed that I would never let anyone (particularly a man) control me and tell me how to live my life.

My family lived a couple of doors down from one of my Dad's brothers who had four kids of his own, one of which I grew up with and spent most of my childhood and young adult-life. My cousin and I went to Catholic grammar school. We were inseparable and always compared ourselves— grades, achievements and looks. I never felt good enough and it played with my self-esteem for many years. I was introverted and never knew who I really was because of the constant comparisons. Life had now become a competition and how I had to prove that I was equal or better than her and others.

After eight years of growing up and going through grammar school, we then went on to the same public high school. High school for me was absolutely horrible. It's supposed to be a time of growth, finding who you are, and having fun with friends. Unfortunately, I found that I ended up depending on my cousin's friendship more than she did mine. We eventually went our separate ways as she "broke the chain" and became more popular while I was still standing in her shadow. Finally, in my junior year of high school, I started to become my own person. I joined tennis and choir and was starting to find myself. I knew that after high school, I wanted to go to college and be independent. My cousin and I went to two different colleges our first year. However, she then transferred to mine. This bothered me initially, but I was older and on a mission. I pursued my undergraduate degree in psychology, joined several honor societies, clubs and became a part of a sorority. I really put myself out there and I soon became more outgoing and confident. *In reality, my cousin and I were like sisters growing up. Even though today we really don't talk and have our own crazy, busy lives, I do think about her and wish her well.*

I had never dated in high school, but, there was something different in college. I went to parties and laughed and felt a part of something. I'm sure it sounds crazy and as I write this it sounds pitiful, but I guess that I was just a "late bloomer". Anyway, I did meet someone, Ted. He was the brother of a fraternity member and we talked at a party one night. I was a sophomore in college and he was a junior in high school (no, I'm not a cougar). But he was cute and, of course, I never dated so I thought I would entertain the discussion.

After that night, I really wasn't interested in him. He was nice, but he was young and I had just met him. As time continued, we would run into each other at parties. One night, we were talking and I gave him my number (he was persistent; I had to give him that). He asked me out and I said yes. We ended up dating for about three months and then he broke up with me. We didn't see each other for a while and I had dated a bit. We saw each other again and he said he was going into the Marines. We became pen pals for a year or so. When he came home on leave, he wanted to see me and I agreed since we had built up a friendship. In the end, he asked me to marry him and I said yes.

I finished undergraduate school and then went on immediately to get my Masters in Management and Organizational Behavior, focusing on my career. In May, 1996, Ted and I got married. We weren't too sure how this "thing" called "life" was going to work. Even though we were "pen pals" for a while, we (or I) really didn't anticipate this next stage in life. It just happened. At first, Ted wasn't too sure of his career path. He thought of becoming a police officer. However, I talked him out of it because I was afraid that he would get hurt. He then became a cabinet maker and I found a Human Resource Manager position.

Our first couple of years were rough as we were still trying to learn about each other. I had some jealously issues, money was a "hot" topic, he was lazy and I had doubts. We argued and I didn't think we were going to make it. This went on for about three years. Then, I got pregnant! I didn't know if I wanted kids. I was on a career path and was focusing on that. I didn't think that I was "mommy" material. While pregnant, Ted and I did get closer, but it didn't last for long.

In 1998, after a C-section, my 8 pound/21 inch beautiful son, Rocco, was born. He was (and still is) amazing and a true blessing. Shortly after he was born, Ted left his cabinetry job and was trying to find himself. He went from job to job for years, which created a burden on me and continued stress on our marriage. It was spiraling out of control. I lost respect and the "mutual partnership" went out the door. In order to take control of our lives, I had to find another job that paid more. My son was six months old and I found that I couldn't enjoy my time with him. I was inundated with work, money issues, maintaining the house, and guilt for not being there for my son. I was now the "husband and wife" and I resented Ted for that. I did find a job and found out after a couple of months that I was getting a new boss. She was very controlling and difficult to work with every day (I couldn't even write an email without her changing it). I would come home feeling upset and talk to Ted about it. However, he didn't understand. This went on for about ten years. Ted and I became "roommates" and loneliness set in for the both of us. We tried to talk but were never on the same page. We even met with a marriage counselor.

Unsure of what to do, we moved a couple of times over the years thinking it would solve our problems. Our last move was to a far western subdivision where we had a house built. There were new families and the hopes of new beginnings. However, after five years there, it still didn't bring us closer. Later that year, December, 2005, my father passed away from Stage 4 kidney cancer. He was only 59.

After almost ten years of working with a controlling boss and no growth, I was given another opportunity that paid more and seemed to allow for further advancement. I actually had two job offers. However, I took the one that paid more knowing the other one would have been better. I had to do what I had to do, right? I wanted control and I wanted to make a career, but, I was going nowhere fast and without much to show for it. Six months after this job, my Mom was diagnosed with lymphoma and I was worried that I was going to lose her shortly after my father. I had to help take care of her, which meant during lunches I had to leave work and then come back and work late. My job was stressful and I had to travel. Ted and I grew even more distant. *In the end, my Mom beat cancer. She ended up learning how to drive and is now independent. She has been through a lot and is a very strong woman.*

It was the end of 2008 and we discovered Facebook. Yes, it seems silly that I bring this up, but as most of us who know, it has its pros and cons as it relates to "old relationships". Since Ted and I weren't talking much, he was on it a lot. One day, I asked him why he kept running upstairs and he didn't answer. I didn't trust him, so I looked in our office and saw that he had been talking with some old high school girlfriend. I blew up and then that was the end. It was a long time coming and we finally divorced in May, 2009. I would always bring up divorce in arguments, but, would never do it. I would use it as a "defense mechanism" when I felt threatened or out of control (and yes, I have "control" issues that I inherited from my father—but not as bad). Ted left the house and stayed nearby with his Mom. He would come back to the house every Wednesday to see our son. I had a long drive home from work and would have terrible anxiety knowing that he would be there. His favorite thing to say to me was "why can't you just get over this and move on". I couldn't look at him and his "smug" attitude ate me alive. I watched my son have fun with Ted, his new girlfriend and her kids and ended up becoming obsessed with seeing hurtful things said about me on Facebook. I was consumed by all of this. I ended up weighing 80 pounds (I'm only 5 feet tall and originally weighed 100 pounds) and unable to live my life. Since I had lost so much weight, my boss called me into his office one day and said people were talking about me. I told him what was going on and tried to "move on", but I wasn't doing very well. I didn't want to seem weak but I asked for some time off (family medical leave). I was gone for a week and then had to go back to work because it was too busy. However, I wasn't ready. After long deliberation, I decided I couldn't stay anymore and resigned. It wasn't the smartest thing to do, but I had to do it for my own health and sanity. *Just to clarify, I did love Ted and we did have some nice times together. However, we were too young and two very different people on a journey that led in different directions. We both contributed to the dissolution of our marriage, and, as of today, we are "friends" and share the same goal which is for our son to go to college.*

A lot transpired between 2010 and 2011. I am now a single mother trying to make ends meet. The house that was built when Ted and I were trying to run away was too big for just two people. I had to sell it and took a huge financial loss.

My son and I moved into a townhouse to rebuild our lives. I had consulted for a bit to bring in money and even tried a new career. However, it didn't pay the bills. I didn't know where to turn. I had some money in reserve and did get some help, but I felt useless and hopeless. I ended up going on food stamps for a while, almost to the point where I thought I was going to be homeless and felt like a failure. I cried most nights praying and hoping for a sign since I didn't know if I could put the fallen pieces of my life back together.

After some ups and downs, I did find a full-time job that lasted a couple of years. It wasn't meant to be long-term, but, just enough time for me to get back on my feet again. This job catapulted me to my next stage in life. It took years of being in the shadows to arrive at a place of growth, confidence, creativity and an entrepreneurial spirit. It led to me to starting up my own consulting business. The next several years resulted in reinventing who I was, being with my son and feeling "human" again. I tried Match.com and dated on and off for a while. Then, when I least expected it, I got a "wink". I met an amazing man, Scott. We dated for almost five years and married in August, 2015. My son and I moved into his house (with his three kids) and we are now a "blended family". I am so lucky that he came into my life. He is the reason I am able to continue my business and achieve my goals. Now, after almost two years, I am still the Owner of LiL-Roc HR Consulting! I focus on organizational development initiatives such as change management, process improvements, training, and coaching.

Although one day I may know the "whys" in my life, I do know now that each "life-event" shaped me into who I am today...and I am grateful. Most importantly, I wouldn't have been able to be where I am without my faith in God and a hope of a new tomorrow.

Lisa Rexroad

As the owner of LiL-Roc HR Consulting, Lisa currently works with clients to help them better understand the current and future state of their people, processes and tools. With over 15 years of organizational development experience, she leverages a combination of strategic thinking, analytical leadership, passion and energy to drive business solutions forward. She has a collaborative, genuine approach with her clients and challenges conventional thought by offering a unique perspective.

Lisa has worked in the marketing, electronics, financial and healthcare industries as a Human Resources/Organizational Development Professional. She has developed strategic HR business partnerships, conducted organizational needs assessments, led change management and process improvement initiatives, facilitated leadership coaching sessions and workshops and has implemented and trained teams on web-based performance management systems.

Lisa earned her B.S. in Psychology and M.S. in Management and Organizational Behavior. She is certified to administer and interpret Hogan Personality Assessments, is an AchieveGlobal Leadership Skills Facilitator and is a certified Team Clock Consultant. She volunteers as a Mentor and Board Member of the Alumni Group at Elmhurst College.

Lisa enjoys spending time with her family, loves hiking, canoeing and travelling.

Lisa Rexroad
LiL-Roc HR Consulting
P.O. Box 5012
Wheaton, IL 60189
630-488-2244
lilrochrconsulting@gmail.com
www.lilrochrconsulting.com

Elizabeth Anthony Gronert
Survive Business Challenges and Learn to Thrive

I had a friend with money to invest. He learned that I was frustrated where I was working as a nail technician. I was a single mom with a toddler and was living with my mother. He offered to be my silent partner in opening a salon. It was an unexpected gift that I was determined to turn into a triumph.

My customers ranged from successful entrepreneurs to stay at home moms. One thing that bothers me to this day, is that not one of these professional women offered to mentor me. I did not have the wisdom yet to know to ask. It is because they all selfishly wanted me to do their nails forever.

The salon was small and humble but we developed a great reputation quickly. We were well-known for our thorough sanitation and disinfection of skin and implements. Our location was not the best, so we were sure to treat each person like gold by employing excellent customer service to be sure that they found their way back to us again.

Not long into my career as a salon owner, I was approached by one of the leading manufacturers to do training with their products—first locally and then nationwide. What was taught on the coasts was not available in the Midwest. During the hours that I was not on stage training, I attended every advanced class possible. Airbrushing makeup and nails was growing quickly at that time. Over a few months, I created a repertoire of samples to show my clients and the nail professionals when I was at the national and local trade shows. This led to my Airbrush Seminars. There was such a large demand for training that I ran the salon Tuesday through Saturday and taught Sunday and Monday. My classes expanded to include artificial nail coatings and natural nail care. This led to The Institute of Nail Technology!

One of my clients, Jackie, offered to provide the financing to build the salon or nail school of my dreams. I was ready for a new challenge and eagerly accepted her financial assistance with the caveat that I would continue to do her nails. When she came one day with paperwork asking me to sign over the shares to my business so that she could have all the tax write-offs, I was so grateful for her financial support that I wanted to do anything to help her. I signed the documents without hesitation, giving her accountant and attorney complete power over what I thought was my business.

As you probably suspected—this did not end well. Her accountant kept giving us "advice" on how to run the business. My trusted business associate, Sandi, started to get suspicious as our figures started to move from in the black to scary red. I mentioned to Jackie that we did not feel that her accountant's advice was working and we were going to go back to what worked before. After a few months, the numbers started to turn back towards black.

Shortly after that, we received a document from Jackie's attorney instructing us to close up the business within 7 days. To say I freaked out, is an understatement. I picked up the phone to call Jackie. No answer. And then I remembered our conversation from the other evening when we did her nails—she would be unavailable on an international cruise for two weeks. The blood began to drain from my head. I sat down and called a past client for a referral to a business attorney. I quickly learned the error of my trusting ways. We later learned that Jackie's other business was having a stellar year and she needed a huge write-off. Talk about attending the University of Hard Knocks! Jackie betrayed me and all the people who worked for her to lower her tax responsibility. Unbelievably, when she returned home from her trip, she called and wanted to schedule her next appointment. Imagine!

This loss really sent my head spinning. However, I started making phone calls to do damage control. After a bit, I moved our offices into my mother's home. In time, I saw that this horrific experience actually catapulted the business into a much more profitable venture. We had been having problems filling classes locally. We were now footloose and fancy free. Progressive Nail Concepts evolved! We could travel to any location and teach.

Three remarkable things happened during this "transition."

First - I started writing for THE publisher for the beauty industry, Milady Publishing. I initially co-authored a few cosmetology books by writing the nail technology sections. I was then invited to write a text book completely on my own—Airbrushing Nails! This text book was not a moneymaker but the credibility it gave me was priceless.

Second—The book made me the official Airbrushing Nails Expert. A leading airbrush manufacturer, Badger Airbrush, asked me to be the artist for two nail videos. (You can still find these videos in airbrush nail kits found at Hobby Lobby and Michaels.)

Third – I was asked to be the FACE of Aztek Airbrush to the beauty industry—literally. My face was on all the airbrush boxes and promotional materials used for that market. I designed the airbrush nail product line of my dreams. I also wrote the script, performed the techniques and directed the development and editing of five videos for Aztek.

With Aztek's support, I trained a team of thirteen people teaching my techniques using the Aztek Professional Nail Airbrush system. My team traveled nationally and I traveled internationally. We attended all professional tradeshows. Something unexpected then happened, Aztek was purchased by a large company. They deemed the professional beauty division not profitable enough. For reasons too crazy to explain quickly, this information did not reach me for three months. By then, I had racked up considerable consultant travel expenses that were never reimbursed. I was again betrayed and left for broke. I went from being a main stage figure signing my books, videos and products to being a single, unemployed mom, now caring for my mother and in six figure debt.

I had no support system around me this time. My pastor saw the change in me and asked me to try a small group. I would have always told you I was a Christian but thanks to this small group of strangers, my life changed forever. Shortly after my faith changed, I found full-time employment working for someone else for the first time since I was a teenager.

I was invited to one of those home party things. Since I traveled internationally, I had few local friends. I had been a home party snob. I didn't have the time and I didn't understand it. I watched the Weekenders Fashion Coordinator do the presentation and thought, I can do this for a while to make some much needed money.

I built a wonderful team of awesome women who were a joy to mentor. I was paid to do something that I really loved – helping people! It was a time of explosive personal growth. I was eventually able to see the devastating loss of Progressive Nail Concepts as a blessing. I had survived two completely devastating life events and was thriving! I realized that God had had a plan for me all along.

Literally, overnight, Weekenders closed. But this time, my third loss of a business completely out of my control, I was able to focus. There was no derailment due to the stress. What was important now? It was figuring out my next step. How was I going to do that? There were four people who came to mind. Three of them were leaders in my Weekenders Company that I admired and the other one had been my business coach. I learned from these business savvy women the importance of negotiating the best deal for the team of women you support and how to compare business compensation plans.

The shocker was how my phone started ringing and the emails came flooding in. People had found out that Weekenders had closed and they were forcefully recruiting. I was also approached by the corporate side of the Party Plan business to see if I would be interested in becoming a company coach mentoring leaders in the field. All of the attention was flattering but I needed to make a decision quickly so I had something to offer my team and customers.

I partnered with the woman who I admired. She had chosen two businesses to build so I followed suit. A third of my team also tried the two businesses or just tried one or the other. Another third said, "I am in mourning —try me later". And the final third of them swore off direct sales forever.

One business was very similar to what we had done before—Jockey Fashions. The other was a completely new world—luxurious bed layers. I enjoyed both businesses but excelled at the Private Quarters luxury bedding. There were many reasons for this. First, my husband, Kris, could work this business with me. It was our retirement plan. The second reason was that my son was struggling with a chronic pain condition; my stepmom had fibromyalgia; and I was in the throes of menopause (such timing!) We built a six figure business helping people sleep restoratively. Over time, my Jockey business became a personal shopping club. Unfortunately, Private Quarters was a young company and after seven short years of not grasping how to be successful in party plan, their investors closed the doors. There was a big difference this time. We knew one month before they closed.

This time I was prepared. I quickly communicated the three things to expect. First, we had the blessing of time to research the next step while continuing to earn. Second, that our phones, email, Facebook Messenger, texting, etc. was going to blow up with people headhunting. Third, the leaders could expect that a third of their people would be able to process this quickly and be able to listen to their thoughts on next steps. The second third would need a longer time to mourn the loss of their business before being approachable. The others would want nothing to do with direct sales—possibly forever.

While my team got busy applying this advice, I started interviewing. One of the benefits of having been in the business for 14 years is that now my database held the names of many who could help. Some were successful leaders like myself. Others were independent consultants and coaches who had their hands on the pulse of Social Networking.

From my survival of past losses, I knew that this was a divine intervention to move us strategically. Being 51, my prayer was not to build another business again. Kris and I created a list of non-negotiables for this next journey. They were things that had to be in place for us to consider the business viable. Before every call I prayed "Lord, I will know which companies to consider because you will fill me with Your Peace." After three weeks of conference calls with over 60 companies, we selected our business partner. (Visit my blog to learn about our parameters.) We left the multi-level marketing/party plan world and started marketing for an online shopping cooperative of a US manufacturer. The business model was simpler for our customers and business builders. It is also willable like a traditional business.

We are now able to enjoy and appreciate this life so much more because of the wisdom gained by the loss of four businesses. I am blessed to be able to assist others who unfortunately have also had to face the loss of their business through no wrongdoing of their own. If this describes you, reach out. Let us help you to navigate your mine field. We are proof that you can survive and likely thrive! We now know that life challenges are a divine course adjustment to alert us that it is time to choose what is next in our unique journey.

Elizabeth Anthony Gronert

Elizabeth Anthony Gronert found the "Man of her Dreams" in 2002. Prior to that, Elizabeth was a single mom for 20 years and cared for her mother in her home for 10 of those years. Elizabeth has chosen careers with a flexible schedule so she can prioritize her husband, children, grandchildren, family and friends. Elizabeth has always operated with a Plan B….well, actually it is now Plan F! Elizabeth loves helping others feel and look their best—inside and out. Elizabeth is passionate about encouraging others to be the best they can be. We know that God wants abundance for us and our families.

With over 30 years of experience owning her own business, Elizabeth is a seasoned trainer, coach and mentor. The first 20 years were in the Professional Beauty Industry as a salon owner, platform educator and international trainer. Elizabeth then transitioned into Social Networking with her first decade in Fashion helping people with Total Image Consulting. Elizabeth entered the health arena by helping people learn how to sleep more restoratively. Elizabeth leverages her knowledge, resources and advocate partners to help people and families be healthy….and live by avoiding ingredients that may be harmful like gluten, grains, dairy, allergens, toxins, and carcinogens. Her goal is to help people learn how to manage their budget and have peace of mind that everything in their home is safe!

Elizabeth is a veteran speaker, stage trainer, published author of textbooks, magazine columns, technical videos and blogs. Elizabeth is an active fundraiser who enrolls others in giving back to the community. Elizabeth and her husband, Kris are on staff at Willow Creek Community Church helping their large church build a mid-size, rewarding community.

Specialties:

- Business Trainer & Social Networking Coach
- Fundraiser for Charity & Community
- Event Speaker employing an Eclectic Range of Experience

Elizabeth Anthony Gronert
Your Comfort For Life
847-502-8394
elizabeth@yourcomfortforlife.com
www.yourcomfortforlife.com

Andrea Banke

Re-Collecting My Marbles; My Journey with Losing my Marbles, Re-Collecting Them, and Healing

I sat in my endocrinologist's office crying. It wasn't the holding it together type of cry where I could blink back the tears, compose myself and force a smile. It was an ugly cry with big fat teardrops streaming down my face and soaking the front of my shirt. Month after month, I saw doctor after doctor and received test after test, and was told each time that I was "fine". I was anything but fine. My built up frustration was spilling uncontrollably out of me. My rain barrel was full, and I could no longer exercise self control. My rain barrel runneth-over, and I wept.

"I feel like I'm crazy." I whispered to my doctor. In that moment, that lovely woman took my hand, looked into my eyes, and said "You're not crazy. I promise you, you're not crazy. We're going to figure this out. It's going to be OK." For that—I will forever be grateful.

I felt like I had lost my marbles and had fallen down. These were feelings I had experienced before at difficult times in my life. Difficulties in life are guaranteed. When things become so difficult that you feel you've lost your way, who you are, and all that makes sense—how do you cope, survive, and heal?

"Pain in this life is inevitable, but suffering is optional." From the first time I heard this quotation, it made sense to me in a logical way, but not in a heart sense. I didn't truly understand it. I'd like to think that at this glorious time of life we call middle-age, I finally somewhat understand, and embrace this concept. It's been quite a journey to this place. Do I feel that I have "arrived"? Not by a long shot. As far as I can see, life is a journey of never-ending lessons. If we pay attention, and work at it, we just might learn something worthwhile. Then we can share what we've learned with others along the way, hoping it will somehow help them too.

My first experience with losing my marbles was when I was eighteen years old and graduated from high school. To say that I was not excited about the future is a gross understatement. I liked high school and my friends. I liked the familiar and was not at all a fan of change. I had lived in the same house in the same town for my entire life. The thought of leaving and going to college rocked my world. However, the thought of staying home and being left behind while all my friends went away to college terrified me even more. So I chose to go away to college. Poorly thought out actions often yield poor results. My fear turned into panic, and panic turned into an anxiety disorder.

Away at college, I was in an unfamiliar place that I did not want to be. I was freaking out daily because I didn't know what was happening to me. I was pretty sure I was either dying of some rare and horrifying disease, or had completely lost my marbles. Neither was a good option. So I did what seemed logical. I stopped going to classes and hid in my dorm room eating peanut butter while listening to Pink Floyd. First semester, two weeks before finals, my worried older sister came to visit me. I cried hysterically, told her I was going home with her, packed up my stuff and went home. My panic and terror were ruling me, and I had few tools with which to cope.

It was 1988, the pre-internet era. Anxiety disorders were an unknown to the general population. Mental health issues still have an unfortunate stigma today, but it was much worse then. I was fortunate to have parents that took me to an excellent psychiatrist who diagnosed me with panic disorder. What a huge relief to know what I was experiencing had a name and that this disorder affected people in all walks of life and in all professions. It was common and treatable. I began to see a wonderful psychologist for counseling who introduced me to meditation through guided imagery. I had friends that stuck by me and loved me no matter how many marbles I currently had, and bit by bit, I healed. Within eighteen months, I had learned about anxiety and acquired tools to manage it. Marbles re-collected, I decided to return to school and enrolled at the local community college.

The first day of class, his adorable self walked in. I straightened up in my chair and thought, *"Who's that?!"* His name was Christian. Apparently, he noticed me too. When the teacher told us to get up and introduce ourselves to someone we didn't know, he made a beeline for me and introduced himself. As we shook hands, I remember looking into his eyes and thinking "He has the kindest eyes I've ever seen."

A year and a half later, we were married. Twenty-one is young to get married but at the time it seemed a good choice…and it was. It was one of the best decisions that I've ever made. Life with Christian was *fun!* He was the most charming, laughter-filled, and entertaining person I've ever met. He had a kindness and gentle way about him that made you feel good just being in his presence. Christian had that effect on pretty much everyone he encountered.

Five years into our marriage, my healthy young husband became shockingly unwell. Over the next five years, he was diagnosed with a kidney disease which required a kidney transplant. He also suffered the dissection of an unknown aortic aneurysm and miraculously survived emergency open-heart surgery to repair it. Three and a half years later, Christian had elective surgery for an abdominal aneurysm and died the day following surgery.

The years during Christian's health challenges were an emotional rollercoaster, but there was also a lot of joy. In the beginning years of our marriage, I suffered two miscarriages. During the five years that Christian struggled with health issues, we were blessed with two beautiful and precious daughters. Despite the challenges and ups and downs, we were a happy family.

Our faith, family, friends, lots of prayer, and love kept us going.

Christian had lived a lifetime with undiagnosed Marfan Syndrome, which is a connective tissue disorder. That is what caused the aneurysms. Christian's father had passed away from an aortic aneurysm but Marfan Syndrome had not been diagnosed at the time. Any child Christian fathered had a fifty percent chance of inheriting it. Our oldest was diagnosed with Marfan Syndrome when she was two. Our youngest does not have it.

When Christian died at age thirty-one, I was a thirty-two year old widow with a four and a half year old and a twenty-one month old. Once again, I lost some marbles.

My grief was so wide, so deep, and so high, that I didn't know where it ended and I began. It was a living breathing thing that accompanied me day in and day out wherever I went and whatever I did. Christian and I had always said we could handle whatever came our way as long as we had each other, and we did. Now it was just me, there was a lot to handle, and I didn't know if I was up to the task. How ironic that I had commented to Christian on more than one occasion how hard parenting was and that I would never want to be a single parent. Hello, single parent.

Re-collecting those marbles took a while. Anxiety was once again trying to be my new best friend. I was confused and surprised to be diagnosed with PTSD, since I had never been to war. The psychiatrist kindly explained that anyone who witnesses trauma, as I repeatedly did over the course of Christian's five years of medical mayhem, can develop PTSD. To work through it, I attended grief class and counseling, prayed a lot, and lived one day at a time.

Two years after Christian's death, I decided to pursue a career helping people who were in pain because I had witnessed him experience so much pain. I considered nursing and massage therapy. I decided "no" to nursing since I am not a fan of bodily fluids. I enrolled in massage school and met amazing people whom I adore to this day. I graduated two years later, became a licensed massage therapist, and began a private practice. During massage school, I learned about many aspects of healthy living and took my first meditation class. I also learned about yoga, essential oils, healthy eating, and began to lift weights and run daily. I thrived while in that healing community.

During the next several years following massage school, I was unaware of the fact that my stress level had built to the point that it had become a daily companion. I struggled to juggle single parenting, running a business, and all of the activities and responsibilities that come with life. My healthy habits of clean eating, regular exercise, and meditation went by the wayside. I stopped taking the time to take care of myself. I was in a long-term relationship that was good, until it wasn't. I learned that even though two people are both good people who love each other, relationships don't always work out the way you want them to when they are also very different people who want very different things.

I slowly lost my health. It was such a slow slide, that I didn't realize it was happening until my body was screaming at me. I never had any allergies and suddenly developed a ton of them. I began having debilitating migraines and a frequent upset stomach. My hormones were erratic, I was having racing heart episodes that were not related to anxiety, and my hair was falling out. I would vacillate between being so wired I could hardly slow my brain down or sleep, and days where my exhaustion was so extreme that getting showered seemed like a monumental task. I was having trouble swallowing and sometimes choking on food. I was a hot steaming mess terrified at what was happening to me, and even more terrified at the thought of not being there for my children. And so began the rounds of doctor visits and tests, while I searched for answers. I was repeatedly told I was "fine", when I knew I was not. My issues were continually chalked up to anxiety once it was found I had a history with it, but I knew it was more. Yes, I was anxious again, because I knew something was very wrong, but was told it was not.

The marbles took off again, bringing us back to the beginning of this story with the ugly cry in my endocrinologist's office. I thank God for her. She diagnosed me with Hashimoto's thyroiditis, an autoimmune thyroid disease. The little gland on the front of your neck is very important. Mine was waging a full out war and causing weirdly terrifying symptoms. I had also had a goiter, or as I liked to call it, fat neck, with three nodules on it.

So, I had explanations. Now, I needed solutions. Medication did not work well for me. Apparently, I'm complicated in addition to sensitive. Upon diagnosis, and for the first couple of years, the goiter was very large, and the 3 nodules continued to grow, to the point that one was biopsied for cancer. I then decided I'd had enough of being freaked-out and paralyzed by my situation, so I did extensive research on what I could do to facilitate healing. Changing my eating habits helped a great deal. Adding in a mindfulness meditation practice further accelerated healing. After three years, the goiter and nodules shrank tremendously. I became calmer and more peaceful than I had been in a very long time.

My children are now in high school with my oldest preparing to graduate and attend college. She was re-diagnosed in grade school with Loeys-Dietz Syndrome which is similar to Marfan Syndrome, and is medically managed. While dealing with her health condition is a necessary part of life, it in no way defines her life or who she is. She has a wide variety of interests and leads a full and active life. My youngest is at the beginning of her high school career and pursues her passions and interests as well. I adore my children more than I can express. I love the strong, motivated, and engaged young women they have grown into. They are my greatest joy, and there will never be a job more important than being their mom.

My career continues to evolve as I do, and I now enjoy teaching mindfulness and meditation as well as providing massage therapy. I look forward to discovering more ways that I can learn and grow, and have additional ways to help and serve others.

Does this mean I think I've got it all figured out and won't fall down and lose my marbles anymore? Of course not, but I do have tools to use when difficulties arise. Faith and prayer have always been my foundation. The addition of a mindfulness meditation practice has equipped me with more tools and greater emotional resilience.

Mindfulness continues to teach me about myself and the world around me, as well as how I relate to myself and the rest of the world. It has taught me how to extend compassion to myself, and to increase my capacity for extending compassion to others. I am grateful for what I have learned about accepting myself and all of my feelings and life experiences—happy *and* hard.

I spent years running away from negative emotions, pushing them down and out of sight, and thinking I had gotten rid of them. Out of sight and out of mind does not mean "dealt with". Mindfulness has taught me to face into the wind of negative and scary emotions and lean into difficult feelings. I have learned that I can experience pain, but I don't have to suffer. I can recognize an emotion and allow myself to feel it, and then I can set it down, choosing to walk away while allowing it to be there. I don't need to force, control, push, pull, or "do" anything with it. I can abide with it.

The point isn't to no longer lose your marbles or fall down. The point is to learn to be OK with falling down, and to keep standing back up and re-collecting those marbles. To learn, grow, and love yourself through it all.

Andrea Banke

Since personally experiencing the mind-transforming and life-changing benefits of Mindfulness and Meditation, Andrea Banke has become a Mindfulness and Meditation Coach who loves sharing the gifts of the practice with others.

In 2006, Andrea received an Associate of Applied Science with Therapeutic Massage Honors from the College of DuPage, and a certificate of completion in a comprehensive 770 hour program in Massage Therapy from the Wellness & Massage Training Institute. Andrea is a licensed and board certified massage therapist with 10 years of experience in the health and wellness industry.

Andrea has completed numerous continuing education courses including certifications in meditation and stress management, and is passionate about the mind-body connection and its significant impact on our health. She enjoys helping others to achieve their health and wellness goals by addressing all aspects of good health. Andrea believes in the importance of life-long learning, and looks forward to continuing to learn, grow, and share with others.

Mother to two teenagers and two rescue dogs, Andrea enjoys digging in the dirt and growing things, meditation, reading, crafting, yoga, movies, laughing, and bacon.

Andrea Banke
Andrea Joy, inc.
630-207-0110
ajoybanke@gmail.com
andreajoyinc.com

Lisa Oddo

Faith is the Backbone to Our Blessings

Everyone experiences highs and lows in their lives to varying degrees. We accomplish great things and make mistakes that teach us important life lessons. It is important to get through each struggle with a happy, thankful heart, and to have faith in ourselves and others. A life of mediocrity is going along day to day living the same way, doing the same tasks, and feeling unfulfilled because it's getting stale. We think, speak, act and react similarly, and magically expect a different outcome. In reality, we know that our situations will not change without our making the necessary changes to our thoughts and attitudes. It starts there. Once we are in a positive mindset, our willingness, energy, and actions can flourish. I used to catch myself not reflecting, but becoming a negative thinker. I would talk myself out of going places, trying new activities, or telling myself that someone else was better suited for it than me. I have learned now to try new tasks within clubs, associations, church and work. By doing so, I have discovered talents that I didn't know existed. I was limiting myself without realizing it and without trying. There are key characteristics to success in every situation.

1) PEACE—This can be found through quieting our minds and bodies through prayer/meditation. Taking the time to speak, process, organize thoughts and ask for guidance will help. This process helps to get focused. It clears the mind of the negative self-talk. Our thoughts and feelings get sorted out too.

2) AWARENESS OF OUR BLESSINGS—We can be thankful for the material items that we obtain. However, we need to remind ourselves that many things are wants and not necessities. Often, one can take for granted basic needs that people in other places can only wish they had. People strive for more stuff-homes, cars, toys, money-bigger, better and best. Are you running rampant to obtain and maintain these items? Is it bettering your life and the lives of those that you love?

3) HANDLING LIFE'S TRIALS—We often fear the difficult moments that we face daily. I was prone to asking myself questions such as, "Am I going to say the wrong things, choose incorrectly, or react poorly?" Notice how negative those questions sounded. We can shape our thoughts and attitudes so that the words and actions reflect positivity. Our character is strengthened throughout the experience. In time, we can show empathy, support and comfort towards others in their times of struggle.

4) REMAINING HUMBLE—It's easy to take all the credit when something goes well in my life. We get excited and want to share our successes with others. I assess my motive before doing so. Ask yourself, "Am I happy or am I simply bragging?" I believe there is a fine line that we need to be cautious about and not to cross. Our successes involve a journey of circumstances, choices, opportunities and other people. We can rejoice in the good times, but be sure to include all of the details.

5) BE THANKFUL—I try to thank people who help me. A hand-written note, small gift, or call is made with specific reasons why I am thankful to them. I am thankful to God for his guidance, care, and love that help me in every situation. I strive to talk with Him about these things every day.

6) HAVING BALANCE—Sometimes we try to put all of our eggs into one basket and our hopes into one area. In this case, I'm talking about putting our time into a topic, task, idea, or even a person. It is vital to keep a balance in all areas of our lives so we don't have burnout. We also want to be inclusive of the people we hold dear to us. Offering our time, effort and communication is a way to show our respect to them. They feel important to you and will be there for you in return.

7) BE BRAVE—Reach out to others to get to know them. You will find similarities with them that you can talk about. This builds a network with others in their fields of expertise and strengths. Try new ideas. This will also open up more doorways for skill-building, relationships, interests, and contacts. Get on a new committee, try a new hobby, go to a new fun place, get to know that neighbor or colleague, and please—volunteer.

I would like to share my personal testimony where the above traits were stepping stones in my growth, both as a young child and later as a young adult. It describes the most difficult times of my life. I often wonder how I made it through them, but I realize that I had a strong support unit of family members and friends by my side.

I was raised in a Christian home with very loving, selfless parents. My mother had this light and fire for Christ and my father really wanted that too. He started attending church with her and then they brought Tony and me with them from the time we were born. We prayed over every meal and before bed, attended services, Awana and youth group.

I was 7. It was an October night, and I was supposed to be asleep. As a little girl who saw her grandparents periodically across the miles, I was excited for their special visit. They were using my room, so I slept on the floor in my brother's room. I could hear unfamiliar voices and lots of movement in the hall as well as in my parents' bedroom. I knew something was wrong, but didn't realize what exactly or how it would change my life forever. Mom was 32 years old when she found a lump in her breast. She was later diagnosed with breast cancer 6 months after giving birth to my brother. She fought hard with a happy heart along the way. I had no idea that my grandparents were there to be with her to say goodbye. My mother lived a little longer than the doctors thought. They gave her 6 months, but her drive and love for us helped her hold on for an additional 4 years. She was organized-specifying instructions for our care and our "tendencies" for anyone watching us on her frequent, days-long stays at the hospital. She prepared the plans for her funeral ahead of time so that the burden wasn't left on my Dad. She encouraged my father to attend church faithfully, and later we went as a family. Her light, drive, and God's love is what caught my father's attention in the first place. He wanted what she had, and even after her passing, he continued to take us to church.

It was in my college years that I fell away. I was busy with my sorority, which in itself focused on academics and spirituality. I focused more on going to parties, drinking, spending time with unhealthy friends—pretty much making mistakes in doing whatever I wanted to do. I messed up. For that, I am truly sorry. I always prayed at night in order to fall asleep and knew that God was listening. I didn't see my behavior at the time as destructive, because my grades were better than they ever had been before. I counted my blessings about being raised in a Christian home. I would occasionally open my Bible at random, point down, and read where my finger hit the page. The meaning behind what I read was difficult to understand, since I really wasn't fully vested, yet I had that need to connect with God.

Shortly after college graduation, I lost my father very suddenly to a heart attack. My entire world crashed down before me. We had gone through the typical difficulties as father and daughter in my teen years, but we had learned how to communicate calmly, lovingly and by listening to each other. When I truly listened, I knew that his words and behaviors were done out of love. At the time of his death, I had only sat down once with him to learn how to keep and balance a checkbook. I still have difficulty balancing it to this very day. Thankfully, the bank tells me I have little bit more in there than my calculations show—usually. I will never forget the call I received just after 9 pm on the evening of February 22, 1994. It was from a gentleman at our health club. My father had been in a racquetball tournament for several weeks. He was tied for 1st place and had an extremely high amount of energy. He would barely sit down before popping back up to attend to a task. I warned him a week before that if he didn't slow down, he would give himself a heart attack. Through all of the active behavior and an intense playoff night, he had one. I remember hearing, "Your dad has fallen on one of our courts." When asked if he was alright, I was told they were transporting him to Elmhurst Hospital and I could meet him there. I didn't know what it meant when they put you in a consultation room to speak with doctors and nurses. I had expected him to sit up, start yanking the cords out, and joke with the nursing staff. It would not be that way. The startling news of his death forever changed me. It forced me to grow up very quickly, take care of a home, get my brother through 3 more years of college, run my dad's business while teaching and become a landlord to a commercial property that had been trashed and abandoned by the tenant, etc. I had to develop thick skin and just get in there to handle one thing after the other. My brother and I wondered if he would need to quit school. Dad put me through school. We had the income coming in that dad did in order to help, so we had the money for him to continue. God had his hand in that situation and he always does. Tony finished school and has a family and a successful business. I am extremely proud of him and thankful for him.

Seventeen years ago, I moved and kept passing Bloomingdale Church for years. I realized that something was missing. I was spiritually separated from God, and wanted to follow His plans for my life. I wanted to walk closer to the Lord, attend church, read the Bible, and learn more about being a better Christian and a better person. I am trying to do that now as I reflect on my thoughts, words, actions and reactions to others. I'm thankful for the teachings, bible studies, and worship through music in ways that I never dreamed of being a part. I am thankful that my parents' faith in God was so pivotal in my childhood and helped draw me near to Him daily in small ways, over and over again in the most difficult times of my life. We are children of God, and He will never leave us or forsake us. He had a plan for each of us long before we were born, and has walked with us all the while. He carries us in our heartaches and strengthens us to carry others. What you say and do for others matters. I will never forget the loving gift of faith that my parents gave to me and how returning to Christ has saved me.

There are people in your life that you influence or will in the future. I encourage you to let Christ's ways take center stage in your daily life. What a difference it will make for you and others who see your life. Even in the difficult times, we can find the peace of Christ that changes us inwardly and on the other circumstances that we are facing. We can trust God in the midst of them.

Lisa Oddo

Lisa Oddo is an educator of children with special needs at the elementary and middle school levels. She has B.A. in Early Childhood Education and a M.T.L. in Teacher Leadership. Her master's project was bound and is available for use at Elmhurst College, where she received both degrees. Lisa has taught children of various ages, abilities, and needs over the past 25 plus years. It is important for her to help each child learn from the academic/social/physical skills and strengths they have and use those as a springboard for growth. She is active at the local and regional level of the Illinois Education Association for the support staff in her school district.

Lisa has always had a passion for editing and writing. She edited Misfortune, a short story that was included in a book of poetry and essays titled Eclectic beyond the Skin. The second writing is a fiction novel with many Chicagoland references, called Relic of the Cross. Lisa has been invited to write a story of her faith journey to be included in a chapter for themed books. She was asked to write the story of the passing of her mother to breast cancer, from her recollections as a child. Many individuals will share their perspectives with the purpose of assisting others with the loss of loved ones to the various forms of cancer.

Lisa is very active at Bloomingdale Church where she is a part of the choir, worship team, Women's Bible study, greeter, usher, nursery helper, and adult education teacher. She is also president of her association board, and a member/past Co-President/Philanthropic Chair/Mayor's Charity Ball committee-Women's Club of Addison. *Your Plan for my Destiny* is a faith-based song that is currently in the works.

Lisa Oddo
663 N. Katherine Lane
Addison, IL 60101
630-935-1395
missoddo@att.net

Gina Sannasardo

Peace and Joy Can be Yours

Hi there. I am Gina Sannasardo. I have recently become a certified Christian Life Coach. I haven't been so excited and passionate in pursuing something like this for a very long time. Thank you for taking a peek at what has lead me to this amazing point in my life! All my life, I have felt a calling to live out my faith. Whether it was revelation, or merely intuition, I knew at a tender young age that I needed to share my message of faith for others to learn about God's abundant love for them. I had a loving family that was strong in their faith and attended mass every week. This foundation continued as I attended an outstanding Catholic grammar school and a terrific public high school. Both afforded me opportunities to learn, grow, and discover who I was a person and how I wanted to live my life. Even in high school, I reflected on how I could be respectful and kind. Was I a perfect, angelic saint? Of course not, but I knew that God loved me anyways, regardless of my flaws and imperfections. There were many difficult times as I grew older. However, I remained vigilant in how God was working in and through my life. There was one time in particular, where I was really being a taught a lesson about being able to accept what I couldn't control. Rather than obsessing about should or could have been, I was prompted to redirect my focus on the "Serenity Prayer." This simple, yet profound message gave me an inner peace that I could not have gotten on my own. I was able to let go and let God. I was also able to accept that although I couldn't control the situation, I was able to have serenity in the idea that "it was what it was". From there, I was able to move on. I was lucky enough to meet my amazing husband Sam at college and to have a fairy tale wedding. Although it all seemed perfect and according to how "everything should go," I was in for some major life changing surprises.

I was blessed to have a beautiful daughter Juliana, who made it very easy for me to experience what heaven was like. The love that I experienced as a mother and the love I received back, really opened my eyes to the unconditional, unlimited, no strings attached, no record of "wrong doings" love that God had for us children of His. As we continued in our family life (as according to plan), we decided it was time to start trying for another baby. Like any other couple, we moved our daughter into the big girl room so that the baby room was made available. We just didn't realize that it would be available for so long. We tried and tried, we were poked and prodded, and tested and examined. We were told that we couldn't have any more children. We were told to "keep trying". We were told something was wrong with me. We were told that something was wrong with my husband.

At this point, getting pregnant seemed close to IMPOSSIBLE! It had been about three years. We also had another trial to endure-my father's incurable, untreatable stage 4 terminal kidney cancer. Since we were inundated with all of the issues with his illness, we decided (okay it was really me) to let go and really, really, without a doubt, surrender to God and trust in Him. This was because all of my prayers and novenas needed to be focused on my dad and not what I wanted -having another child. My dad really suffered more from emotional afflictions than anything else at first. He wondered "why him" and relentlessly believed that it was typical for him not to catch a break in life. He suffered from major depression and finally his illness had really taken a toll on his physical state.

His cancer spread throughout his body, and in less than a year his body was no longer able to keep up. We had been told his disease was aggressive, but slow. However, due to his emotional state, he deteriorated much more quickly than anticipated. He was then paired up with a hospice nurse in our home to which he finally surrendered his life into God's controlling hands.

He sought peace, harmony, and reconciliation with us and God. After much prayer and faith, my dad sadly passed on. However, he also went into Jesus' loving embrace in heaven. How do I know this? It is because of St. Therese of Lisieux. That my friend is a surprise story (miracle really) that you will have to check out on my website!!

Since my father died, leaving my mom the house to care for with a troubled knee, we believed it would be best to have her move in with us. We had an addition built to the house, had some financial strain, worked on the dynamics of this new relationship with my mother and us, and we were on our way. All this time, I still secretly in the deep depths of my heart, wanted another baby. It wasn't that my daughter wasn't perfect for me. However, a mother's heart knows when another baby is waiting. I still quietly prayed, cried, mourned, and had faith in God that everything would work out. Since my daughter was now in school full time, I wanted to get a job. This helped alleviate the "obsession" and hurtful preoccupation of carrying this heavy cross that I told God I would hold for Him in order to help be redemptive and save souls as my St. Therese did. I read a prayer that stated that God doesn't say no, but rather yes, not now, or I have something else in mind.

I believed that my job was the "something else in mind". I really came to love my position as an 8th grade Language Arts teacher. As I took to the position, I then read another prayer that said I would get paid for something I really had a passion for instead of volunteering for it. At this time, I had been volunteering with my husband as an 8th grade religious education teacher. When all this happened, I truly believed that it was much better for me to be following God's agenda and not my own. Even though I had received many hurtful comments from people as to why I "didn't want" to have another child, I quietly humbled my anger and would calmly tell them we were having trouble. After about two years, I finally felt content about not having another baby. I really learned to savor my precious rose (that is what I called my daughter). I also had many friends and family pray for me and St. Therese was in action again (I cannot divulge the whole story here, but it is on my website).

I finally found out after 7 years that we were going to have a baby!! YEA—and we all lived happily ever after...almost. We had typical sibling squabbles from my two children that drove me bananas and the usual married couple's spats, etc. etc. We had been living our daily lives with routines to be kept, schedules and tasks to be completed and the usual business we all get caught up in. However, the "caught up in", began to feel like "STUCK" for me. As a result, I started to forget who I really was and became angry, depressed, tired, annoyed, and lost. I had no desire to think about the future. I focused on daily survival with minimal time to breath. At least, that was the way that it felt. My husband always told me to breath. I would anxiously hold my breath and couldn't escape the cycle. Peace and joy were not to be mine.

Although I knew that Jesus was always there embracing me and my beastly ways, I needed help. My son had just been diagnosed with Crohn's disease at the age of 4. It is a chronic life-long inflammation of the digestive tract. In his case, the colon was bleeding as well as other problems. With added expenses to hospital bills, natural remedies, and all organic, non -gmo, no gluten, soy, dairy, low sugar (the list goes on) food, my stress levels became too much to bear. My mood swings affected everyone in the house including my marriage.

My life became a vicious cycle in which I was crabby and tired, took it out on my family, then felt horrible amounts of guilt for being a bad mother, wife, daughter, etc. I hated looking in the Parent magazines since I never felt that I matched up to those expectations in order to be a better "Supermom." At this point of feeling rather low, I prayed to God, "What do you want me to do?" "What do you want me to do?" I really didn't know what to do, but my God DID!

The very next day, I received an email on life coaching. I had never seen or heard of it before. However, I was prompted to look into it. Talk about the Spirit moving. I knew right away this was something right up my alley that

I could really be good at. The admissions director was really patient with me as I picked her brain with many questions and different scenarios. I called my husband and he agreed that this was an invitation from God calling me into greatness. I enrolled into coaching school at iPEC and began not only learning about these terrific and amazing paradigms, theories, and practices, but really found the ideals and beliefs to be complimentary to my belief systems. I knew that this confirmed what I loved to do, which was to share my message.

From this experience, I have gained friendships, bonded with amazing people, gained confidence in myself, been able to recognize the gifts in others that they couldn't clearly see, and deepened my trust in God's divine plan for me. I found what I was seeking: harmony, peace, joy, happiness, fulfillment, and purpose. The energy has been contagious! I wouldn't say it if it wasn't true. However, life coaching has changed my life. I know that it can change yours. I know how to broaden my message I have always shared in a more insightful, creative, and accepting manner.

My transformation has come strictly from God and from the angels with which He has surrounded me. His love as allowed me to live my life how I want to live. Peace and Joy are now my reality and valued beliefs, not just for myself, but for all to have. I am learning and using coaching breakthrough methods to which I view life with a new perception. I view trials as opportunities for growth, knowing that I CAN choose how I look at life, feel about the situation, respond vs. react to my environment, and make changes that honor who I want to be and how I want to live.

This has allowed me to be free to trust in God so that I walk on the path He set for me. It is a path where I am more in control of my being and doing. My faith has been my be all and end all.

I will strive to help you find what might be blocking you from getting you where you want to be, assist in obtaining actionable goals, enable you to rediscover your talents and gifts, and help create the life you want to be in. Thanks so much for taking the time to learn about my journey and how

God has allowed my life to be transformed when I trust in the Holy Spirit's movement.

I can partner with you to help feel God's plan for you come alive as He did for me so that Peace and Joy could be yours!! Let's transform your life together!! God Bless!

Gina Sannasardo

Gina has been happily married for 16 years to a fantastic, giving man named Sam. They have two wonderful children: Juliana age 14 and Peter age 5. She is a Christian Life Coach who wants to partner with teens and adults struggling with finding their real "who" so they can find peace and joy in their daily lives. She is a Certified Professional Coach (CPC) with an ELI-MP from the Institution of Professional Excellence in Coaching (iPEC), an ICF coaching institution. She has a Masters in Education (M.Ed) with a focus on Language Arts from University of Illinois at Urbana-Champaign (UIUC). She is also a full-time middle school Language Arts teacher for St. Philip the Apostle School. In addition, she has a B.A. in Education. She has been blessed to have been afforded many opportunities to have seen the Holy Spirit move in and through her life. She is excited to start her next chapter in life...God Bless!

Gina Sannasardo

Peace, Joy, and You

1520 W. Jo Ann Lane

Addison, IL 60101

630-677-2649

gina@findinggodspeace.com

www.findinggodspeace.com

Marianna Guenther

It's Quite Simple: I Didn't Say Easy

My heart is pounding with excitement. I am finally here! I can hardly wait to get off the bus that took me from Bratislava, the capital city of the small country of Slovakia, across the ocean and all the way to London, England. I am here and the excitement is now almost unbearable. I take a deep breath. Is that how the air smells and tastes in London?

The bus is parked next to a small Indian shop. As I look at advertisements taped to the window glass, I see different spices, food items, and saris. I pull one of the ads off of the glass and make my way to a red phone booth. I saw myself making that call from that red booth hundreds of times in my dreams before and now it's reality. My heart is beating superfast and now I think it might actually explode and make a big huge mess on the sidewalk. I am so ready for a shower, a clean shirt and a nap. But first things first. I am here and about to get a job, live in London and learn English! It's for real!

I dialed the number and forty-five minutes later I am sitting in a red car with the two cutest little boys. They look like angels except that their hair is dark brown. I just became a nanny! I can't contain my excitement. How did all of this happen? Dreams do come true, quoting one of the Disney princesses.

Just short three months earlier, I came across this 'great' idea of learning English by actually living in an English-speaking country. Even though I was accepted and attended high school for diplomats, took twelve hours of English each week and was being taught by American teachers, I still wasn't speaking fluent English after a year at it.

Yes, there were many people who told me I was crazy and that I would never get a visa allowing me to leave and travel. This was even though the country was moving away from Communist censorship. The Velvet Revolution happened in 1989 and it was now 1995. I was young and broke. I was not exactly a model example of someone who would be allowed to travel. The Slovakian government would never issue a visa to someone like me. I sort of knew that, but I wasn't focusing on it. I was busy making money so I could afford a one-way bus ticket to London. Against all the odds, I got a stamp in my passport. Now, how do I tell my parents?

I am here, in London! Here is the Tower Bridge (which is different than the London Bridge). As we drive by the River Thames, I see Westminster Abbey and Big Ben in the distance. I answer a few questions about my trip and whether I am hungry. The next thing I know, we're here - in Edgware, a district of north London which I am about to call my 'home' for the next year or so.

By now, I am starving. Since I am not able to explain that I am a vegetarian, I have no choice but to gobble down a ham sandwich. Oh, well, another thing on tomorrow's agenda. I think I will live.

I grew up in Eastern Europe. I had just a few outfits to get me through the week. I wore leaky boots to school in the wintertime. We didn't have buses to take us. I just changed my socks once I got there so I wouldn't have cold, wet feet all day. I know it doesn't seem like reality to some people. This is especially true given that I am only forty one years old and stories like these are something that our parents and grandparents used to share with us about their lives. But for me, it was just a short twenty-three-or-so years ago.

Another of my memories is that we used to only have bananas at Christmas time. I still love to take a nice big sniff of an orange. It's smells like Christmas to me and reminds me so much of my childhood. It re-affirms that it's okay and that it was okay. I am okay to have left all that I knew. This includes my mom, dad, older sister, younger brother, baby brother and my best friend in the whole wide world. My baby brother was only three back then.

He probably thought that I was just going to school and I'd be back on Friday just like I had done for the past year. Somehow, I knew that he'd be okay too. I knew that leaving all that behind would be worth it and that I must follow my dreams. I trusted my gut, although I didn't know what was on the other side. But grass is not greener on the other side either. Grass is greener where you water it. I didn't know what the reward was yet, but I wasn't worried about it.

My goal at that time was simple. I wanted my children to have a better life than I had. I wanted them to have many choices, freedom, autonomy and the ability to become whomever they wanted to be. That's what learning English meant to me back then. I did realize, years later, that we all have a purpose on this Earth. We are all here for a reason and we all have an obligation to give back by becoming more. The truth is that, by continually learning, we grow which allows our gifts to be shared with the world and make it a better place for all.

Little did I know that two years later, I would now make a similar journey to the United States. This time, I travelled in style. It was my very first flight! Everyone who I dared to share my vision with, warned me that I would never get a visa since I had a Slovakian passport. Even flight lieutenants were concerned that I would not be allowed past the gate.

However, against all the odds my feet touched the U.S. soil. I felt the freedom in the air! I can't explain it. However, it was as if I grew wings. Did you ever have a dream in which you are flying, not on the plane... but like you're literally flying? That's how it felt.

Once I got here, I travelled and saw thirteen states during my first summer. It was awesome! It was overwhelming how huge the country was. Just driving from Phoenix to the Grand Canyon put things in perspective, especially for someone who comes from a country of five million people.

I was having a lot of fun but kept my vision in the forefront. I realized that a college degree might not be such a bad idea. Once again, my 'unreasonable' goal was met with resistance and skepticism. 'This would be almost like studying in a foreign language', 'which is hard' and 'you didn't finish high school in the U.S.' so 'you might need GED'…blah… blah…blah…

I said: bring it on! I graduated with a B.S. in Finance and two years later, I earned my MBA. Long story short, there were other difficult 'things' that I've overcome - like giving birth to my first son whose labor lasted seventeen hours and who weighed nine pounds and one ounce. It has also included a successful corporate career that I enjoyed for over fifteen years.

Then one day as I commuted to and from the Chicago suburbs to my job downtown, I noticed people on train who looked like zombies. They seemed to have no life and no emotions. I then realized that I was one of them, I was a zombie too! I did the same thing every day and didn't know why I was doing it. I didn't have any passion and I had lost my purpose. In fact, I was becoming a person I didn't even like. I wasn't proud of what I was doing, who I was becoming and how my actions were affecting other people's lives.

Yes, I was able to provide a great lifestyle for myself and my family. However, I was miserable most of the time. I was not fun to be around. It was something that… I felt like… I needed to change. I needed to get back to my authentic self. However, I had lost touch and I didn't know how to get it back. The truth is that I've reached my goal! I lived a life of my dreams! I enjoyed and experienced life. I have traveled to wonderful and beautiful countries and places.

But the true breakthrough happened for me. It was not until one late evening, when I worked with my team on a project in my office. I totally forgot to make it to my son's school orientation that evening. I broke a promise to my son. I knew then that I wouldn't remember what I was working on with my team late in my office that night but I knew I would remember a promise I broke. I remember breaking out crying in front of my team. It was at that moment I realized the impact my decisions had on my life. I had an empty feeling inside. I recognized that I was an example of a perfect failure. I had "it all" but I was not balanced. My life wasn't balanced. Most importantly, I wasn't living my own authentic mission.

But how can I leave all this behind and put my family through this? What if we lose it all and my kids will have to live under the bridge? What if we become homeless? All these crazy ideas were running through my mind. It was insane!

For those of you who have kids, you might be familiar with a book: Where the Wild Things Are. As these irrational pictures were flashing in my head, I remembered a story about a boy named Max who felt distance from his mother. His bedroom underwent an enigmatic transformation into a jungle environment. He sailed to an island inhabited by malicious beasts, the Wild Things.

I thought about what would happen if my kids were to ask me later in life: "Mom, how come you stopped living your dream?" What would I say? "Hey kids, it's because I wanted to make sure you're taken care off." How would I feel telling my kids that they are the reason why I settled? Ouch!

The truth is that it was about me and my insecurities. I was scared. The fear was just too great. I was scared to leave what was too familiar and too comfortable. I was afraid to walk into the unknown even though I had done it time and time again. I had just forgotten. It was time to remember. It was time to wake up!

I started with the basics. I asked myself: "What drove me in my life to achieve great results?" I then asked myself: "How can I continue to succeed and be authentic with who I am while having joy in my life?" The truth is that all the thinking is… it is a process of asking and answering questions. If you ask a better question, you get a better answer. If I asked myself: "Why am I so miserable?" I'd get: "Because you're a bad person." That's not helpful! I'd already felt that way.

The interesting thing is that all the answers are within you. There is so much information out there. In fact, we're drowning in it. You can Google anything within a matter of seconds. Right on your phone! It's amazing!

However, it's also disruptive and even destructive. For me, at the risk of sounding a little bit of woo-woo, sitting quietly and meditating or filling myself with gratitude, happiness and joy and aligning my heart and mind is where answers live and solutions appear.

The answer that I'd received when I asked: "What drove me in my life to achieve unbelievable results," was simple: hunger. So how do I re-light that fire that pulled me to get over that ocean and into the unknown? It's by knowing what I wanted. I've always had that almost obsessive vision. It was something that pre-occupied my mind constantly until I got it. It was going to England and learning English, travelling throughout the U.S., marrying the guy of my dreams (that would be a fun story to write, I literally stalked my husband into dating me), becoming a U.S. citizen, graduating from college, making well over six figures, zip lining in St. Lucia, swimming with stingrays and dolphins in their natural habitat (the best ever, Anguilla). I always knew what and why I wanted it. I had a purpose that drove me no matter what the obstacles or the failures.

That purpose is as strong today as it was back when I was a little girl climbing the trees in my parents' backyard. It was also against my grandpa's advice for me to be cautious because I could fall down and break my arm or leg. "Do you see me grandpa? I yelled from the top, "I didn't break anything." I am a rebel by nature. At first, I didn't do things on purpose to prove others wrong, but as time went by, I've learned it's something that works. Defying the odds, challenging the authority, questioning the rules and standing on the side of the underdog… works for me. It was no wonder that I didn't 'fit in' to a communist culture that teaches you to be a good sheep and follow the herd. It is in contrast to an American culture that strongly values the ideals of entrepreneurship, independence and self-reliance. Smiley face. You can't deny that there is something bigger than you and I. It is something that guides our lives and watches over every step we take.

I manifested from the Universe and as always, the Universe delivered.

My company announced a voluntary separation program. Since I had a super understanding boss, I left my corporate job in June 2015.

Unlike Max, I didn't want to undergo that journey. However, what I then recalled is that Max, after successfully intimidating the creatures, became the king of the Wild Things and delighted in a romp with them. When all was said and done, Max decided to return home, to the Wild Things' disappointment. Upon arriving in his bedroom, he discovered that a hot supper was waiting for him. When you step into the unknown, and you succeed, there is a reward. There always is a reward. How wonderful!

In fact, our mind is two million years old. Its primary function is survival. Our brain is not here to make us happy. Our mind makes unrealistic, super scary and false representations of what may happen if you ever get out of your comfort zone and wander into the unknown. However, that is its job! None of those scary deceptions ever come true!!! What our mind makes us imagine, never happens. Sadly, some of us may never know if we don't take that first step.

Let's fast-forward just a bit. In one short year, I got closer to my kids than ever! I have my own business. I ran in the Chicago marathon. I became and got certified as a Life and Success Coach, Clinical Hypnotherapist, Reiki Practitioner... The list goes on. I am also about to become a published best-selling author!

So, what's next? No matter where my journey takes me, whether it's being a speaker or an author sharing my vision and inspiring millions of people, or your coach helping you accomplish your dreams and transforming your life, or being an employee working for an awesome business... for someone wonderful and sharing my gifts with their clients so they can continue to innovate making this world a better place for everyone to live in... Staying flexible and trusting the Universe to guide me... being authentic and true to whom I am and having joy every day... is what I am about.

My sincere wish is that our paths cross in one way or another sharing my gifts with you, serving you, and helping you to reach whatever you're striving for so you can then share your mission with this beautiful world of ours.

Marianna Guenther

Marianna Guenther is a Peak Lifestyle Strategist and founder of Athletezy, Inc. She helps her clients and audiences realize their dreams and potential by challenging the status quo, defying the odds, bending the rules, and living their lives on their own terms.

After spending over fifteen years in corporate finance sharing her gifts and knowledge with globally recognized industry leaders, the Universe guided her to pursue a path of becoming an author, speaker and life and success results coach, while she stays flexible. Marianna's passion is to help people to create real change in their lives and to realize for themselves that change is neither hard nor long. In fact, all that's required is our ability to ask the right questions, listen and take the first step.

She is a firm believer that how you feel every moment is more important than what you do or what you have. Knowing what's possible in life when you commit to your vision and pursue it with 100% passion, anything is possible.

Living her ideal lifestyle is important to her instead of working to survive life. Marianna and her husband, two awesome, athletic and good-looking sons, and her dog Champ enjoy an active, healthy and busy lifestyle.

Marianna Guenther

Athletezy, Inc.

marianna.guenther@athletezy.com

Sheri Sauer

If You Are Going to Work in a Man's World, You Better Grow a Pair

My story starts in 1999, when my life was turned upside down. I had just left my marriage with three children, ranging in age from three to five. I did not know my destiny or how I was going to make it. However, the time came for me to get away from a husband who could not break his drug habit. I was no longer going to let my children grow up in the toxic atmosphere that we called home. I loaded up the car with as many belongings as I could gather and we went to stay with my parents. I am very thankful that I had my parents to help me through these very difficult times. I don't know how I could have done it without them.

My three children (who did not know what was happening) and I were all together in one room. We had no idea what the future held for us. I had many things going through my head. I knew that I had to find an attorney, a new job, new schools and eventually a new home. It was all very overwhelming, to say the least. All I could do was pray and take things one day at a time. I went to work on hiring an attorney. Once I found him, I told him my story. He said that based upon the drugs, the mental abuse, a special video that he had taken of himself, as well as all of the marital counseling that we had together, it was clear that I would get a quick divorce and sole custody of my children.

Well, he was half right. However, there was another problem. My youngest son did not talk. It was feared that he might have been sexually abused or he had seen my ex-husband making the videos of himself. I was devastated and again felt hopeless. I took him to the doctor to get examined. There were no clear signs of any abuse. They sent us to a therapist for an evaluation. The therapist found that he was very angry. However, we did not know what he was angry about. During this entire period, my ex-husband repeatedly dodged being served the divorce papers. They were finally served and he refused to sign them. In addition, he would not let me into the house to retrieve the rest of my belongings. Even though my name was on the house, it still had to be approved by the court. Every time we went to court, I begged to have access to my children's belongings along with my personal things. The court process took so long that I finally got into the house on my own and hired a mover to move me within six hours before he got back. I was afraid of him and his threats did not help.

I asked for supervised visitation. However, in the court system that was not a high priority. The divorce needed to be completed before the visitation would be looked at. My ex did get only daytime visits every other weekend which I was thankful for. Meanwhile, I still needed to take care of my youngest and make sure that he was OK. We went to the therapist weekly. I also reached out to a wonderful organization called LADSE. They did a home evaluation on my children. They said that my son had gone through something traumatic. However, at age three, it was hard to say what that was. After a year and a half, the divorce was finalized. I did receive sole custody but we had to continue the fight for supervised visitation. That required more time in the court system.

Not too long after the divorce, my attorney passed away. That meant starting over again and finding a new attorney. They needed to hear the story again. The attorney that I found specialized in these cases. She assured me that she could get the visits supervised, so back to court I went!

During this period of the court proceedings and therapists, I found a job working in a little restaurant as a waitress. This worked out great for me because it was the early shift. It allowed me to be with my children most of the day. I could also pick them up from school. This was not my forever job.

However, it took care of the bills. I was always there at the end of the day to pick them up and put them to bed at night. Those days went by quickly (kindergarten, first grade and second grade). It just sped by. During this period, I was still in court fighting for supervised visitation and wondering if it would ever end.

My ex's visits with the kids were very unpredictable. Sometimes, he would come to pick them up. At other times, he was a no show. When he did take them, they came back upset because he would either cut their nails or their hair. He also wouldn't tell me if they got sick or wanted to come home. All of this was documented. However, the judge still did not grant the supervised visitation. It was all very horrible, to say the least. All I could do was pray that they came home safe.

After two and a half more years in court, I was finally assigned a "guardian of lightem" who told the judge that my ex and I should go to a counselor. They said that we had different parenting styles. I was furious but I went. My ex showed up high, so I never went back. I cannot tell you how disappointed I am in the justice system. I feel that it's broken. However, you have to keep fighting for what you believe in and never give up. My attorney was also disappointed. I had two choices. I could find another attorney or I could focus on making sure that my children were safe and well-taken care of. I chose the second option.

As time went by, he came to pick up the kids less and less. Even though it broke my heart to see them disappointed, there was a part of me that was glad they were safe with me and I did not have worry for those few hours. By the time they were in their teens, he never really came around at all. It was sad that they grew up without a father. However, I put so many positive role models in their life that I feel it all turned out for the best.

Every day while I was working at the restaurant, three men came in at the same time. One owned a plumbing company, another owned an electric company and the third was the owner of a construction company. They all asked what I really did for a living. I found humor in that question. It was as if they could see into my mind. One day, the man who owned the construction company offered me a job helping him with his business. He wanted me to schedule clients and to help with marketing and bookkeeping. I thought about it and said yes. I could do this part time from home which would allow me to spend more time with my children.

Within a year, the business grew and I was asked to work more hours. My waitress gig became part time. It allowed me to work full time from home growing the construction business. I found this business to be very exciting. Every day was different. As my children got older, the school hours became longer. This gave me time to visit job sites and to learn the business. It also allowed me to meet with customers to help plan their projects. I loved working with people and learning about the business. The contractor opened an office and I became a full time employee. I was finally able to leave my waitressing career.

I was back on my feet again. Although my children were still young, I could be there to see them off to school and also be there at the end of the day for dinner, homework and bedtime stories. Within the next year, I was able to rent a home near where I now live. My oldest son was in the 5th grade, my daughter was in the 4th grade and my youngest son was in the 3rd grade. They transitioned well to the new schools. They made many new friends on our block. They also kept up the relationships with all their old friends. They stayed in the same Cub Scout group so they weren't disrupted too much. We had band concerts (since they all played instruments), sports camp outs and many other activities that kept everyone busy. I was very thankful for our new surroundings.

As I grew more educated in the construction industry, I realized that I really enjoyed the design process and working with kitchen design. I would take the clients to other showrooms where we would make selections and get a design rendition. I remember thinking to myself that this can't be hard! I also asked many questions. I soon bought the 2020 design program. It was a large investment at the time. However, it was worth it if I could create my customer's dream kitchen. I went to classes to learn the 2020 design program and joined the National Kitchen & Bath Association (NKBA) which offers design courses to become a certified Kitchen and Bath Designer.

By the time my children were in high school, another opportunity came my way. I met someone at a Chamber of Commerce networking event who had a family member in the kitchen and bath business in another state. He made the introductions and I was given the following offer. If I opened a showroom, I could purchase the cabinets through him. All I needed to do was to find a location, buy my displays and take on the company name of True Source Cabinets. I talked it over with my contractor. He thought that it was a great opportunity. I opened "True Source Cabinets". In the beginning, it was challenging to create a new market. I was told to only sell to contractors and designers following his business model. That is what I did. I never signed any paperwork, which I found odd. I could never understand why I needed to purchase the cabinets through him when they came from the manufacturer. I understood that he got a cut in the deal. However, since I was new to the business, I was a little naïve.

Three and half years later, I found out why this was not such a great opportunity after all. I remember it well. It was right before Thanksgiving when I told Mr. True Source that I was going on my own and would be closing my location. That's when the next crazy thing took place. He was so angry that he came at me with a vengeance. He used my company e-mail address and wrote people pretending to be me. He even wrote to my Rotary Club and said some nasty things. I had many people calling to ask if I was OK. When I told them the story, they could not believe that anyone could be so cruel. He continued to do more and more terrible things. He tried everything to put me out of business. However, I told myself that if I could go through what I did with my divorce, I could get through anything. I prayed that the nightmare would end.

In 2011, I left True Source Cabinets to open Premier Design & Cabinetry in La Grange Park. It was a struggle at first. My contacts thought that I had gone out of business. I also had Mr. True Source coming after me. I got through it and I am still standing today. As a result of this experience, I am a better and stronger person. I have always had the original contractor by my side. He has been a rock for me during my darkest hours. I have many people in my life to thank who have gotten me through some very difficult times.

Let's get back to my children. My oldest is a graduate of Northwestern University and has moved into his first apartment. He has a job as a consultant in Chicago. My daughter is at Augustana University, majoring in Biology. She will graduate next year. My youngest son is at Marquette University in the NROTC program. He would like to become a Navy Seal. I am so proud of my children. I cannot say enough about them. They are so special. I believe that God has put them here to do great things in this world. I let them know that every day.

My sons are proud Eagle Scouts and my daughter has been involved in "Venturing Scouts" which is offered to girls at the age of 14. I owe much to scouting and the many great leaders that we have had the privilege to know. We have been involved since my oldest was 7 years old. I have been an active volunteer in many roles for most of our years in scouting. I have even received the prestigious Silver Beaver Award. I have tried to live my life and raise my children using the Scout Laws. I believe that integrity is one of the most important things we have. I also believe in giving to others as so many have given to me. I have overcome mediocrity over and over again in a man's world. It has made me stronger as a person and has brought with it success. As painful as it has been to write this story, I hope that it helps just one woman out there. Be strong and know that there are so many here to help.

Sheri Sauer

Sheri lives in La Grange Park with her two dogs, Red and Patience, and she has three children, but has an empty nest during the school year. She is the President of the La Grange Park Chamber of Commerce and a member of the La Grange Rotary. Sheri also participates in a drug coalition in Lyons Township and is a Eucharistic Minister for her church. She also has a Meet-Up group for women in the construction industry. Sheri loves helping others connect and grow their business. She also enjoys meeting new people.

Sheri Sauer
Premier Design Cabinetry & Tile
1018 E. 31st, La Grange Park, IL 60526
708-372-2579
sheri@premierdesigncabinets.com
www.premierdesigncabinets.com

Jodi L. Suson

Informed Choices

A person dies every 19 minutes from prescription drug overdoses[1], informed choices matter, your life matters. Our lives can take many pathways and you know that the journey can be a challenge. I am sharing my story to make a difference in the world. At the time, I did not understand why I was experiencing so many health challenges. I have been trying to understand for decades. For as long as I can remember, I had a hard time processing and I had brain fog. I often felt like I was in a drugged out sleep. These things coupled with pain, plagued me throughout grade school, high school, college and as I completed my MBA. More importantly, I did not tell anyone. Nevertheless, I was very active in gymnastics, weight lifting, and horseback riding. As a child, I remember my father making protein shakes for me for breakfast. In my early thirties, I used to weigh 125 pounds and bench-pressed 185 pounds. I once took 2nd place in a bench-pressing contest in the late 1980's. But…I was in pain. For as long as I can remember, I had been in pain. For many years, I "reasoned" the pain away. In high school, I remember my feet, ankles and knees hurt so badly, I reasoned, because I was a gymnast.

In 1996, I went to a physical therapist after falling down on the ice in a parking lot in West Des Moines, Iowa. She told me, "the pain is all in your head, and there is nothing physically wrong with you." The pain that I felt was in my shoulders, neck and the levator scapulae.

I was told to see a psychiatrist, which I did. This doctor misdiagnosed

---

1 http://www.drugfree.org/news-service/prescription-drug-abuse-results-in-one-death-

me with bipolar disorder and schizophrenia. I had read that people who had bipolar disorder had a lot of pain, so I trusted what the doctor told me to do. I took the medicine he prescribed for 19 years. I should mention, that I had low self-esteem, which is why I did not question what he or other people told me. I was also looking for a quick fix to my problems. After the first two weeks of taking these medications, I gained over 50 pounds. Eventually, I gained a total of 110 pounds. I weighed in at 234 pounds, which is considered to be obese. The medication also numbed most of my feelings. Even after I started taking the medicine, while the original source of the pain had been minimized, severe nerve pain started in my feet, arms, hands, and even my skin felt like it was on fire. The experience of the "all over pain" is referred to as diffuse pain. I also found that many medical doctors and other professionals get annoyed when you tell them the pain is all over. They tend to think you are less credible.

The doctor that I saw for over 19 years prescribed all of the "new" medications that came out on the market. He also offered to put me into his clinical trials so I would not have to pay for the new drugs. Since funds were tight for me, I agreed to participate in the clinical trials. The issue was that after he put me on one medication, he never took me off any of the previous ones. As a result, I was on as many as 17 different medications simultaneously. Consequently, in 2007 the organs in my body started to shut down. It felt like my brain would switch off when I was sleeping, resulting in incontinence in bed. It did not even wake me up. I just woke up the next the morning cold and wet. When I told my doctor, he laughed and said, "I usually get up out of bed and go to the bathroom when I have to go." He was not only making light of my situation, but he was not addressing the root cause of my problem. Doctors take a Hippocratic Oath to first do no harm.

In 2013, my pain was out of control. My stress levels were completely off the charts. I was having several panic attacks each day. I was grieving the loss of both my parents.

At the end of 2013, I went on disability because of multiple diagnoses that prevented me from working full time, and my employer did not want to provide reasonable accommodations. Despite the fact that I could not work, I enrolled at Lake Forest Graduate School of Management and graduated with my MBA with a specialization in Organizational Behavior in June 2016. In my Business Analytics class, my professor, Steve Rudnick, said, "If someone gives you the mean, but not the median or the mode, you need to ask why?" When he shared this, I was sitting there with braces on both hands because I had just had steroid injections in all my digits and my wrists. I thought to myself, "Yep, you're right, I need to start asking harder questions and dig deeper when talking to my doctor." In addition to the pain, I would experience what one doctor called periodic paralysis. Right after eating certain foods, my body would shut down and I could not move. I recall that many times over the years, I would have to pull over to the side of the road and would pass out cold for hours at a time. I would sleep in the parking lot in my car until I could drive again. My gratitude goes out to Steve Rudnick for opening up my eyes. He reminded me that I have a voice and I should use it.

Next, I confronted my psychiatrist and said, "What we are doing is not working. We need to do something completely different. If you cannot help me, please refer me to someone who can. I cannot get a glass of water to my mouth without using both hands. This is not bipolar disorder. People with bipolar can still move." The psychiatrist referred me to a rheumatologist. I called for an appointment and was told that this doctor did not accept my insurance. However, his associate did and she could help me. I didn't ask the office personnel if this associate was a rheumatologist because I assumed she was. However, I found out after the fact, that she was not a rheumatologist and her action plan was to have me do a sleep study and give me more drugs. I wanted to know the root cause of the problem, not to mask it with more pills as I had done for the last two decades.

So, I had to find another doctor. The journey wasn't pretty. Suffice it to say there was a lot of mediocrity to be found along the way. These particular doctors were mediocre because they just didn't care, or they were only going through the motions. By this time, my approach to working with the medical community had shifted. I was no longer afraid to ask the hard questions. I took the same approach as if I were shopping for anything of value. And nothing is more valuable than your health. So now, if the professional that I am talking to does not listen, or understand what I am trying to achieve…I walk away. Simple!

When my mother was alive, I used to take her to a fabulous neurologist, Dr. Andrew Gordon. In addition to having ovarian cancer, my mother had arthritis and Parkinson's disease. Through my mother, as a guide and as an angel in heaven, I became reconnected with Dr. Gordon. Dr. Gordon listened to my story, the long history of pain, and, of course, he knew about my family history with neurological diseases. After performing various tests, he was able to unravel the mystery and piece together how he could help. I owe so many people thanks for guiding me to better health. But I would not have been writing this story today if it were not for Dr. Gordon. He was the first doctor to listen and care. It was good timing. My pain had finally gotten the best of me and I knew that I did not want to live this way. And…if had to be this way, I did not want to live.

Dr. Gordon's associate, Dr. Aaron C. Malina, PhD, then put me through a neuropsychological test. He discovered that my impaired processing was from pain. I did not have bipolar or schizophrenia. He referred me to Dr. Michelle Kukla, PsyD who showed me how to manage pain drug free. However, it was important to me to make sure that I did not have these mental disorders and that I understood the "why". So I found a checklist on the Internet for signs and symptoms of bipolar, and together with Dr. Kukla, we reviewed each line item. I made sure that I understood what each of these symptoms meant and how that would show up for me. On December 16, 2014, I began the doctor-managed process of getting off all of my medications. I still had many issues. The MRI showed a diagnosis of two torn rotator cuffs that appeared to be 20 years old. In addition, I had developed carpal tunnel syndrome (both wrists), trigger fingers (both hands), a bone spur (right hand), small fiber neuropathy, PTSD and high anxiety. In addition, I was obese. All of these conditions contributed to the pain. However, that day and going forward, I chose to manage the pain, instead of it managing me. Dr. Kukla shared many methods and introduced me to alternative healthcare practitioners who showed me how to let the body heal itself. This experience is what led me on my path to share real health and wellness to our world and to encourage people to make informed choices. I often will add the hash tag #informedchoices to tweets and other social media to reinforce my message.

On my journey, I learned about various holistic modalities for healing and managing pain. I learned about meditation, acupuncture, chiropractic, essential oils, applied kinesiology, to name a few. It is my passion to help people get out of pain and to find wellness. I am committed to creating awareness for others so they can make informed choices about their own health.

I have also learned that synthetic medication is not a long-term solution. It actually masked the root cause of my issue for nearly two decades that allowed my condition to continually degrade; it left me with long-term negative side effects. Instead of taking 20 years from my life, it was really like taking 40 years because, instead of being untreated, I was being mistreated, and that takes its toll on the body. The organs in my body rejected all of the synthetics, including the boxed food I was consuming. My solution was to find a doctor specializing in differential diagnosis, which is the process of differentiating between two or more conditions that share similar signs or symptoms.

Fast Facts: People are Dying

This terrified me enough to take action. "More people died from drug overdoses in 2014 than in any year on record. More than six out of ten deaths involve an opioid. Since 1999, the number of overdose deaths involving opioids (including prescription opioid pain relievers and heroin) nearly quadrupled. From 2000 to 2014, nearly half a million people died from drug overdoses." https://www.cdc.gov/drugoverdose/epidemic/index.html

Having this new awareness set me in motion. I never took opioids, which was just a stroke of luck. But many people do and they deserve the right to know about the holistic and natural alternatives.

In 2015, I learned that one of the drugs that I was taking for almost 20 years contained fluoride. It is a neurotoxin, which we suspect heavily contributed to the Small Fiber Neuropathy that I have now. Knowing that our water supply has added fluoride, I bought special filters as a first step to eliminating toxins in my water. I then removed the chemicals from my home. I stopped eating refined processed foods including sugar, gluten, grains, and caffeine (it aggravated my nerve pain). That was a chore because I first tried to find foods in the grocery store that did not contain sugar. As a result, I became an official "label reader". I then discovered that if I wanted to omit sugar from my diet, I would have to shop the perimeter of the grocery store. Almost all of the food that I consume now does not come in a box or container. I modified my lifestyle and choose to cook whole, organic, or responsibly produced, non-GMO foods. There are a few exceptions to this change. One is a minimally processed food by Miracle Noodle that makes noodles and rice out of the Asian Konjac plant which has amazing health benefits. I consume these nearly every day. The other is Kevita, which is a sparkling probiotic drink that supports digestive and immune health. My choice has been to sustain an anti-inflammatory diet.

On January 27, 2016, I was blessed when my friend Seth Holzwarth introduced me to Dr. Danny McLane of ADIO Chiropractic Clinic in Libertyville, IL. Seth introduced me after I had shared with him my business plan to bring Chiropractic Led Onsite Care to Corporate America. That day was a game-changer. Remembering this literally brings me to tears of gratitude because without Dr. Danny, I would not be where I am today. Dr. Danny is my soul brother. I immediately knew when I met him that we were going to partner to bring real health and wellness to the world, not disease management. Dr. Danny first needed to help me regain my health. Dr. Danny can solve problems in minutes that other practitioners can't ever solve at all. He is much more than a chiropractor. He also specializes in applied kinesiology, neuro-linguistic programing, acupuncture, hypnosis, massage, reiki, nutrition, essential oils, anti-inflammatory diets, and meditation. The list is endless. He removes the interference so the body can heal itself. I have made tremendous progress in my health because of him.

On my journey, I also was having serious inflammation issues. I would break out in hives nearly every day, usually at night before bed. I would actually bleed from scratching so hard. I decided to have food sensitivity testing done that identified over 107 different foods and chemicals that were causing inflammation. In addition, I learned about symptoms of having a leaky gut and the brain-gut connection. If you are interested in learning more about this, there are various articles and books written by Kelly Brogran, MD, David Perlmutter, MD and Josh Axe, DC. These people are all great resources. As of August 2016, I removed all 107 inflammatory items, and started making bone broth soup. The trick I learned was to add apple cider vinegar that draws the nutrients and healing compounds like collagen from the bones that are helping to heal my body. Dr. Danny then started me on the right supplements so that my body can continue to heal.

Today, as I write this, the hives have dissipated. I still itch some, but it has only been about four weeks. It is generally a 9-month process. I have also lost 76 lbs., and I have 33 more pounds to lose to achieve my personal weight goal of 125 lbs.

However, the real achievement is not the weight loss. The real accomplishment was having the courage to challenge the thinking of the "experts" and to think outside the box. It was uncovering the root cause of my problem and choosing not to accept the status quo. My success is sharing with you today what happened... and why. Don't be afraid, like me, to ask the hard questions. If something in your gut tells you that what you are hearing doesn't make sense, keep searching for an answer that does. Make an informed choice.

Today, I work with Dr. Danny as his Chief Relationship Officer and as the CEO of WHP Onsite in Libertyville, IL. Together, with his dynamic team, we are doing a grass roots campaign to share our vision, take people out of pain, and help them achieve real wellness. He does this without prescribing any medications, and instead focuses on removing the interference so the body can heal itself. Everything he does is backed by science.

For me, there are no coincidences in life. Looking back, I see how blessed I am to have lived through this and feel compelled to share my story. As you read this, I encourage you to find your voice if you have not already done so. In the end, my wish for you is to also make your choices, "informed choices."

Passionately yours,

Jodi L. Suson
#informedchoices

Jodi L. Suson

    Jodi L. Suson, The Champion of Informed Choices, passionately delivers outstanding guidance on health and wellness. She is a Certified Corporate Wellness Specialist. She uses her skills to direct a team of experts that connect patients to the best health care providers for their condition. Her position as CEO of WHP Onsite and Chief Relationship Officer to ADIO Chiropractic Clinic in Libertyville, Illinois allows her to connect corporations to professionals to solve the obvious health care needs of their workforce. Jodi honed her prowess at building and growing relationships during her course of study at Lake Forest Graduate School of Management, in the MBA program in Organizational Behavior. To connect with Jodi, please reach out to her on LinkedIn to address the concerns you may have about corporate wellness or your own health needs. (LinkedIn Profile) http://lnkd.in/n67Whr

Jodi L. Suson
ADIO Chiropractic Clinic
WHP Onsite
316 Peterson Road
Libertyville, IL 60048
847-738-0242
jodi.suson@WHPOnsite.com
www.ADIOclinic.com
www.WHPOnsite.com

OVERCOMING
Mediocrity©

Now interviewing authors for our next
Overcoming Mediocrity book.

It's time to share your Super Hero Story!

www.DPWNPublishing.com